Lenin

T0345309

Titles in the series Critical Lives present the work of leading cultural figures of the modern period. Each book explores the life of the artist, writer, philosopher or architect in question and relates it to their major works.

In the same series

Lenin

Lars T. Lih

REAKTION BOOKS

Published by Reaktion Books Ltd
Unit 32, Waterside
44–48 Wharf Road
London N1 7UX, UK

www.reaktionbooks.co.uk

First published 2011
Reprinted 2011, 2018, 2022

Printed and bound in Great Britain
by TJ Books Ltd, Padstow, Cornwall

British Library Cataloguing in Publication Data
Lih, Lars T.
　　Lenin. – (Critical lives)
　　1. Lenin, Vladimir Ilich, 1870–1924.
　　2. Revolutionaries – Soviet Union – Biography.
　　3. Heads of state – Soviet Union--Biography.
　　4. Soviet Union – Politics and government – 1917–1936.
　　I. Title II. Series
　　947'.0841'092-DC22

ISBN 978 1 86189 793 0

Contents

Lenin, faced with new technology for spreading the word, seems somewhat nonplussed (March 1919).

Introduction

On the shelves of my study, in serried ranks of blue, stand the 55 volumes of the fifth edition of the works of V. I. Lenin. In their way, these volumes – equipped with a fantastically elaborate scholarly apparatus detailing every name, book and even every proverb mentioned by their author – are the building blocks of an intellectual mausoleum comparable to the corporeal mausoleum that still stands in Moscow. Just as impressive an accomplishment of what might be called embalming scholarship is the multivolume *Vladimir Ilich Lenin: Biograficheskaia Khronika*, consisting of over 8,000 pages detailing exactly what Lenin did on every day for which we have information (usually he was writing an article, issuing an intra-party protest, making a speech).

And yet the very title of this *biokhronika* points to a biographical puzzle, since the name 'Vladimir Ilich Lenin' is a posthumous creation. The living man went by many names, but 'Vladimir Ilich Lenin' was not among them. Posterity's need to refer to this man with a name he did not use during his lifetime gives us a sense of the difficulty of capturing the essence of this passionately impersonal figure without mummifying him, either as saint or as bogeyman.

What should we call him? He was christened, shortly after his birth in 1870, as Vladimir Ilich Ulyanov. 'Ilich' is a patronymic, meaning 'son of Ilya'. And yet, for many during his lifetime and after, 'Ilich' conveyed a greater sense of the individuality of the man than 'Vladimir'. As soon as he started on his revolutionary career in the early 1890s the exigencies of the underground led our hero to distance himself from his given name. The surviving copy of his first major written production – *Who are these 'Friends of the People' and How Do They Fight against the Social Democrats?* (1893) – has no authorial name on the title-page. In works legally published in the 1890s our hero adopted more than one new name: K. Tulin or (for his magnum opus of 1899, *The Development of Capitalism in Russia*) Vladimir Ilin, a pseudonym that hardly hides his real name. Right up to the 1917 revolution, legally published works by Vl. Ilin continued to appear.

Even in a legally published newspaper an underground revolutionary had to exercise care so that his identity would not serve as an excuse to fine it or shut it down. One such paper was the Bolshevik *Pravda*, published in Petersburg from 1912 to 1914. A close colleague of Lenin, Lev Kamenev, later recalled that in order not to compromise this newspaper 'Ilich changed the signature to his articles almost every day. In *Pravda* his articles were signed with the most diversified combinations of letters, having nothing in common with his usual literary signature, such as P.P., F.L.-ko., V.F., R.S., etc., etc. This necessity of constantly changing his signature was still another obstacle between the words of Ilich and his readers – the working masses.'[1]

Our hero acquired his 'usual literary signature' around 1901, while serving as one of the editors of the underground newspaper *Iskra*, when he began to sign his published work as 'N. Lenin'. Why 'Lenin'? We have already seen a certain fondness for pseudonyms ending in *-in*. But 'Lenin' seems to have been the name of an actual person whose passport helped our man leave Russia in 1900. This passport was made available to Lenin, at second or third hand, as a family favour; in the end, he did not have to use it.[2]

'N. Lenin', not 'V. I. Lenin'. His published works, right to the end, have 'N. Lenin' on the title-page. What does the 'N' stand for? Nothing. Revolutionary pseudonyms very often included

Title-page of *What Is to Be Done?* (1902), one of the first publications bearing the name 'N. Lenin'.

Что дѣлать?

Наболѣвшіе вопросы нашего движенія

Н. ЛЕНИНА.

„Партійная борьба придаетъ партіи силу и жизненность, величайшимъ доказательствомъ слабости партіи является ея расплывчатость и притупленіе рѣзко обозначенныхъ границъ, партія укрѣпляется тѣмъ, что очищаетъ себя"... (Изъ письма Лассаля къ Марксу отъ 24 іюня 1852 г.).

Цѣна 1 руб.
Preis 2 Mark = 2.50 Francs.

STUTTGART
Verlag von J. H. W. Dietz Nachf. (G. m. b. H.)
1902

meaningless initials. But when N. Lenin became world famous, the idea got about that N stood for Nikolai – an evocative name indeed, combining Nikolai the Last (the tsar replaced by Lenin), Niccolò Machiavelli and Old Nick. In 1919 one of the first more-or-less accurate biographical sketches in English proclaimed its subject to be Nikolai Lenin. President Ronald Reagan was still talking about Nikolai Lenin in the 1980s – and perhaps this name is just as legitimate historically as 'V. I. Lenin'.

In any event, Lenin never used 'Vladimir Ilich Lenin' as a signature. Most of his letters are simply signed 'Yours, Lenin' or the like. Certainly Lenin did not bother to hide his real name. In a

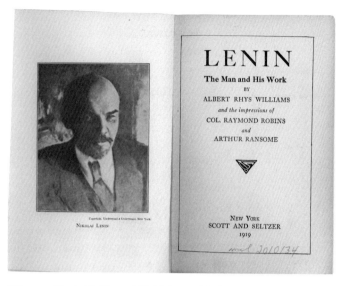

LENIN

The Man and His Work

BY

ALBERT RHYS WILLIAMS

and the impressions of

COL. RAYMOND ROBINS

and

ARTHUR RANSOME

NEW YORK
SCOTT AND SELTZER
1919

Copyright, Underwood & Underwood, New York.

NIKOLAI LENIN

Title-page of *Lenin: The Man and His Work,* one of the first informed accounts of Lenin in English.

1908 letter to Maxim Gorky signed 'Yours, N. Lenin,' he gives his Geneva address: 'Mr. Wl. Oulianoff. 17. Rue des deux Ponts. 17 (chez Küpfer)'.[3] Only in letters to his family and to Inessa Armand does he usually forego his usual literary signature and sign off as V. U. or V. I.

After 1917, when signing official documents in his capacity of Chair of the Council of People's Commissars, Lenin evidently felt that his family name was necessary, and so his official signature on government decrees was 'Vl. Ulianov (Lenin)'. Other revolutionaries whose underground *klichki* (pseudonyms) became famous did not retain their family name in this manner – certainly not J. V. Stalin (born Dzhugashvili).

It seems that our subject, for reasons both personal and official, fought to maintain a distinction between Vladimir Ilich the person and Lenin the political institution. Posterity's insistence on yoking together 'Vladimir Ilich' and 'Lenin' bespeaks not only

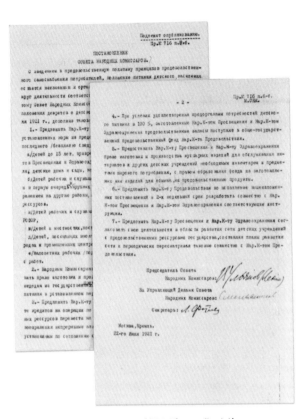

A Soviet government decree signed 'V. I. Ulyanov (Lenin)'.

convenience but also the difficulties of comprehending the shifting demands of personal and political identity in the politics of the Russian revolution.

When we look at the overall evolution of English-language studies of Lenin since the Second World War, we observe a pendulum shift from 'Lenin' to 'Ulyanov' – that is, a shift away from seeking the essence of this historical personage in his formal doctrines and towards seeking his essence in his personality. In the first decades after the War scholars elucidated the doctrine of

'Leninism', consisting of a series of propositions about the role of the revolutionary party, imperialism, the state and even such topics as philosophical materialism. To this end they concentrated on texts that might be called 'Lenin's homework assignments'. Works such as *Materialism and Empirio-criticism* (1908), *Imperialism, The Highest Stage of Capitalism* (1916), and *State and Revolution* (1917) all reflect the diligent note-taking of a writer who feels compelled to make a case concerning a subject with which he is relatively unfamiliar. In fact, several volumes of Lenin's complete works are devoted exclusively to the notes he made in preparation for these books.

Even in the case of Lenin's seminal work of 1902, *What Is to Be Done?*, scholars were much more interested in drawing out what they saw as the doctrinal implications of some of his passing polemical remarks than in the real heart of the book, namely, Lenin's attempt to inspire underground activists with a heroic vision of leadership. In this way scholars used Lenin's homework assignments to construct an elaborate doctrine entitled 'Leninism' and then proceeded to contrast their creation with 'Marxism', concluding that Lenin was an innovative, indeed revisionist, Marxist theoretician.[4]

Starting in the mid-1980s the Soviet archives began to be opened and a new portrait of Lenin emerged. Paradoxically the opening of the archives, so immensely beneficial in other areas of Soviet history, led to even further decontextualizing of Lenin/ Ulyanov. Research proceeded on the (possibly unconscious) assumption that newly declassified documents would unlock the secret of the *real* Lenin. Yet these new documents were themselves highly selective, and for an obvious reason. What sort of Lenin documents would the Soviet authorities keep under lock and key? Obviously, those documents that created problems for the official Soviet interpretation of Lenin, and in particular for the carefully cultivated image of his impeccable virtue and humanity. Keeping back these documents was a crime against scholarship, but not quite as intellectually vulnerable as the creation of a portrait of Lenin based on these documents alone. Oliver Cromwell insisted that his portrait should include 'warts and all'. Post-Soviet studies of Lenin often seem to be based on a methodology of 'nothing but warts'.[5]

The spotlight was now on the quirks of Ulyanov rather than the doctrines of Lenin. Much interest was excited, for example, by Ulyanov's sex life. Books with titles like *Lenin's Mistress* appeared.[6] His political life was reduced to a number of shocking statements, mostly from the time of the Russian civil war, in which he demanded energetic repression. Sometimes it seemed as if the whole vast drama of the Russian revolution and its tragic outcomes were caused by one man's intolerance and cruelty. Even the major large-scale biographies by Dmitri Volkogonov and Robert Service showed little understanding or even interest in explicating and contextualizing what was, after all, one of Ulyanov's central claims to fame: the political outlook associated with the writings of N. Lenin.[7]

The aim of the present biographical essay is to keep the focus on both Ulyanov the flesh-and-blood personage *and* his rhetorical creation, N. Lenin. This is all the more necessary because *the ideas of N. Lenin cannot be understood apart from the emotions Ulyanov invested in them, and Ulyanov's emotional life cannot be understood apart from the ideas associated with N. Lenin*. (Having used the distinction between 'Lenin' and 'Ulyanov' to make this fundamental point, I will henceforth revert to the normal usage of referring to the historical personage by his most famous penname.)

In early 1917 Lenin wrote to his close friend Inessa Armand that 'I am still completely "in love" with Marx and Engels, and I can't stand to hear them abused. No, really – they are the genuine article.'[8] We should take this statement as the literal truth. Lenin was truly in love with the ideas of Marx and Engels. In similar fashion, the most fraught, long-lived and emotional relationship of Lenin's life was his changing attitude toward the most distinguished Marxist of his generation, Karl Kautsky – or rather, with Kautsky's writings.

But can a formal doctrine, with generalized propositions connected by logical implication, inspire such love? Not in Lenin's case. His emotional fervour was inspired by a *lifelong scenario* by means of which he interpreted the eventful world around him. The key theme of this scenario was *heroic class leadership*. The theme of class leadership had two levels. First, most fundamentally, leadership *by* the class – that is, the Russian proletariat's leadership of the whole Russian people, made up predominantly of peasants. *Narod* is the Russian word for 'the people', and (like *Volk* in German and *le peuple* in French) it has an emotional force completely lacking in the English noun 'the people'. For Lenin the urban proletariat was only one part of the *narod*, but a part to whom history had given a special mission of leadership.

The centrality of this theme to Lenin's outlook was brought out by his widow, Nadezhda Krupskaya, in her eulogy after Lenin's death in 1924. The Russian word used here for 'leader' – *vozhd* – is a key term in Lenin's rhetoric throughout his life:

> His work [in the early 1890s] among the workers of Piter [St Petersburg], conversations with these workers, attentive listening to their speeches, gave Vladimir Ilich an understanding of the grand idea of Marx: the idea that the working class is the advanced detachment of all the labourers and that all the labouring masses, all the oppressed, will follow it: this is its strength and the pledge of its victory. Only as *vozhd* [leader] of all the labourers will the working class achieve victory. . . . And this thought, this idea illuminated all of his later activity, each and every step.[9]

Lenin also had a romantic view of leadership *within* the class. He sought to inspire the rank-and-file activist – the *praktik* – with an exalted idea of what their own leadership could accomplish. In

What Is to Be Done? (1902), he challenged his opponents: 'You brag about your practicality and you don't see (a fact known to any Russian *praktik*) what miracles for the revolutionary cause can be brought about not only by a circle but by a lone individual.'[10]

The party inspires the workers with a sense of their great mission to lead the *narod*, and the proletariat then carries out this mission by inspiring the *narod* to join the workers in their crusade to overthrow tsarism, thereby opening up the road that ultimately leads to socialism – this is Lenin's scenario. Thus the two levels of heroic class leadership are interconnected, as eloquently described by Robert Tucker, one of the few scholars to fully grasp the essential content of what Lenin himself called his dream:

> To understand Lenin's political conception in its totality, it is important to realize that he saw in his mind's eye not merely the militant organization of professional revolutionaries of which he spoke, but the party-led popular *movement* 'of the entire people'. The 'dream' was by no means simply a party dream although it centred in the party as the vanguard of conscious revolutionaries acting as teachers and organizers of a much larger mass following in the movement. The dream was vision of an anti-state popular Russia raised up by propaganda and agitation as a vast army of fighters against the official Russia headed by the tsar.[11]

Lenin's scenario was heroic, even grandiose. For Lenin, anyone who failed to share his exalted sense of historical events was a 'philistine'. The Russian language has a rich vocabulary for attacking philistinism – not only *filisterstvo*, but *obyvatelshchina*, *meshchanstvo* and *poshlost*. Lenin constantly deploys this vocabulary in his polemics, mainly against other socialists.

The aim of the present biographical essay is to outline Lenin's heroic scenario, show both its complexity and its thematic unity, reveal the source of Lenin's emotional attachment to it and document its changing role at each stage of his career. The concise format of the Critical Lives series is ideal for this purpose: any shorter and the life-long role of the heroic scenario would be obscured, any longer and the underlying unity of Lenin's outlook would be similarly obscured. These goals impose a strict focus that determines what needs to be said and what (with great regret) has to be left out for the present. My ambition is to bring out a recurring *pattern*. Once this pattern is perceived, it will easily be recognized by anyone who picks up Lenin's writings and reads more than a few pages.

My view of Lenin is not particularly original and chimes in closely with most observers of Lenin in his time as well as with a strong minority of post-war academic historians. Nevertheless, this view does clash on many points with what might be called the standard textbook interpretation. The central theme of the textbook interpretation is Lenin's alleged 'worry about workers'. According to this account Lenin was pessimistic about the workers' lack of revolutionary inclinations and was therefore inclined to give up on a genuine mass movement. He therefore aimed instead at an elite, conspiratorial underground party staffed mainly with revolutionaries from the intelligentsia. Following from this, the textbook interpretation sees fundamental contrasts between Lenin and the rest of European Social Democracy. They were optimistic, he was pessimistic. They were fatalist, he was voluntarist. They were democratic, he was elitist. They were committed to a mass movement, he was conspiratorial.

In reality Lenin was driven by a highly optimistic, indeed romantic, scenario of inspiring class leadership that had strong roots in European Social Democracy. My scholarly self would like nothing better than to fully document this fact and provide extensive back-up for any disagreements with the mainstream. My writerly self realizes that such digressions would subvert the

A May Day celebration in 1919 juxtaposes the man and his official image.

goals of the present book. I shall therefore restrict myself to inform-
ing the reader when I have said something that many experts will
find surprising. A full scholarly defence of my interpretation can
be found in writings listed in the Select Bibliography.

Only when we have a feel for the emotional glue that bound
Lenin to his ideas will we be able to appreciate his life-long commitment to a heroic scenario of inspiring leadership. This scenario is
the profound link between a passionate individual and his public
persona – between Vladimir Ilich Ulyanov and N. Lenin.

The Ulyanov family in 1879. The children, from left to right, are Olga, Maria, Alexander, Dmitri, Anna, Vladimir.

1

Another Way

If a historical novelist had come up with Lenin's genealogy, it would seem very contrived. The intention of the author would have been too obvious: to give Vladimir Ulyanov ancestors from all over the Russian Empire and from as many of its ethnic groups as possible. Among his grandparents and great-grandparents there are Russian serfs from Nizhni-Novgorod, Jews from the shtetls of Ukraine, Lutheran Germans from the Baltic and possibly Kalmyks (a people of Mongolian origin) from the lower Volga.

Looking at the life trajectories of these remarkable individuals, another theme imposes itself: the pathos of the 'career open to talent', individual social mobility, advancement through education and professionalism. This aspect was well brought out by Albert Rhys Williams in 1919, in the first factual biographical sketch of Lenin in English:

> In some accounts he is the 'son of a peasant'; in others he is the 'son of a nobleman'. Both statements are correct.
>
> In old Russia, a man who became a senior captain in the navy, a colonel in the army or a Councilor of State in the Civil Service automatically attained the rank of the nobility. Lenin's father came from peasant stock and rose to the position of Councilor of State. So Lenin is referred to as the 'son of a peasant' or the 'son of a nobleman' according to the animus of the writer.[1]

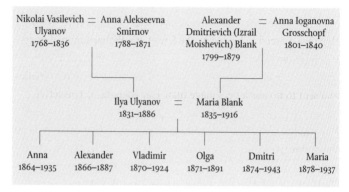

| Nikolai Vasilevich Ulyanov 1768–1836 | = | Anna Alekseevna Smirnov 1788–1871 | | Alexander Dmitrievich (Izrail Moishevich) Blank 1799–1879 | = | Anna Ioganovna Grosschopf 1801–1840 |

Ilya Ulyanov 1831–1886 = Maria Blank 1835–1916

| Anna 1864–1935 | Alexander 1866–1887 | Vladimir 1870–1924 | Olga 1871–1891 | Dmitri 1874–1943 | Maria 1878–1937 |

Vladimir Ulyanov's immediate family.

Lenin's grandfather on his mother's side, Alexander Blank, had already received noble or gentry status as a result of his impressive professional work as a doctor. Alexander's father Moishe, Lenin's great-grandfather, had grown up in a Jewish shtetl in Ukraine and managed to get out after long and bitter disputes with his co-religionists. He educated his own sons in Christian schools and finally, after the death of his religious wife, was baptized in 1835, taking the name of Dmitri. His efforts to rise up in the world had been noticed by some high-ranking bureaucrats who served as god-parents to his two sons. And so it was that Alexander Dmitrievich, the offspring of the shtetl Jew Moishe/Dmitri, was able to hear Anna Grosschopf play the *Moonlight Sonata* and propose to her soon after. Anna's family was representative of the Baltic Germans who had long served the tsar as a source of Western professionalism.

In Soviet days Lenin's Jewish ancestry was a state secret. Lenin's sister Anna discovered these facts doing archival research on her family in the 1920s (not through family tradition). In the early 1930s she personally asked Stalin to publicize the fact as a way of combating popular anti-Semitism in the Soviet Union. Stalin categorically refused, and the facts only became established in the *glasnost* era and after.

Today, Lenin's Jewish genes are no longer the source for scandal that they seemed to be during the Soviet era. Perhaps more damaging to his family's reputation is a remarkable letter of 1846 written by his great-grandfather Moishe/Dmitri when he was in his nineties and sent to no less a personage than Tsar Nicholas I. This letter shows the dark side of all this striving to get ahead: dislike of and contempt for those left behind. Lenin's great-grandfather denounced the prejudices of the Jews, blaming the rabbis for Jewish backwardness. He suggested that the tsar prohibit the Jews from hiring Christians to perform essential tasks on the Sabbath, as a way of gently coercing the Jews into conversion – just like the coercion used to make a sick person take medicine. 'I now hope that our Sovereign Emperor will graciously approve my suggestion, so that I, an old man of ninety years, with death and the grave before my eyes, will live to see the Jews freed from their prejudices and delusions.'[2]

Social advancement on Lenin's father's side was equally impressive. Lenin's grandfather Nikolai managed to rise out of serf status somewhere around 1800. His wife, Anna Smirnova, might have been a Kalmyk freed from serf status and adopted as an adult by the Smirnovs (although this part of the story is not certain). Their offspring Ilya got his diploma from Kazan University in 1854 and, it is said, the great mathematician Nikolai Lobachevsky encouraged him to pursue an academic career. But Ilya Ulyanov became a teacher and then an inspector of schools, with a special interest in setting up the village schools that spread the possibility of advancement through education. In his own family he and his wife Maria Alexandrovna were committed (unusually for the time) to complete equality of education between their three daughters (Anna, Olga, Maria) and their three sons (Alexander, Vladimir, Dmitri).[3]

Thus the Ulyanovs achieved noble status, but did so through all the bourgeois virtues: diligent training, hard work, a focused career and a credo of usefulness. One might look on the Ulyanovs as a success story, a Russian version of 'log cabin to house on the hill'.

Surviving Ulyanovs in 1920. From left to right are Vladimir, Maria, Dmitri, Nadezhda Krupskaya (Lenin's wife), Georgy Lozgachev (Anna's adopted son) and Anna.

But it was precisely their commitment to education and social advancement that put the family dangerously close to a high-tension wire in tsarist society. The tsarist state desperately needed these serious, inner-directed, upwardly mobile professionals but it was also scared of and distressed by them. They upset the orderly traditional organization of society by rank and *soslovie* (legally defined statuses for peasant, merchant, town-dweller, nobleman). They carried the stealthy virus of invidious comparison to Western Europe. They demanded a freedom of action that the autocratic system could ill afford them. They were never satisfied and seemingly could turn extremist at any moment. So Russia built schools for them and then harassed and irritated them. It invited them to serve the fatherland and then treated them like wayward children.

Vladimir Ilich Ulyanov was born in 1870 in Simbirsk on the Volga (Simbirsk was renamed Ulyanovsk in Soviet times and remains Ulyanovsk to this day). For most of his childhood he was isolated from these tensions and thrived in an atmosphere that combined intense application and individual expression. Once a teacher had difficulty carrying on a conversation with Vladimir's mother because Vladimir was running all over the house as a Red Indian, screaming at the top of his voice. 'Children are supposed to scream', the mother told the teacher.[4] But as Vladimir entered his teens, the tensions of the outside world began to close in on the family.

In 1881 the subversive potential of education and social mobility was confirmed when a handful of young intellectuals successfully assassinated the Tsar Liberator, Alexander II, who had emancipated the serfs twenty years earlier. In the new reign of Alexander III, the government immediately took fright and began clamping down on the education system. The new attitude was best expressed in 1887 when a circular from the Minister of Public Education stressed how dangerous it was to give education to 'the children of coachmen, servants, cooks, washerwomen, small shopkeepers, and persons of similar type'. The government now felt safer giving its support to obscurantist church parish schools rather than to the village schools to which Ilya Ulyanov had devoted his career. This steady erosion of his life's work helped bring Ilya to the grave in 1886 at the early age of 55.

The following year the contradictions of Russian modernization struck the Ulyanov family with an even more devastating blow.

From Worms to Bombs: 'Another way, Sasha'

During Soviet times, a workman trying to find a better solution to some difficulty might say optimistically 'Well, we'll go another way, Sasha'. The Sasha of this semi-proverb is Alexander Ulyanov, Lenin's older brother, who was hanged in May 1887 for his participation in a plot to assassinate Tsar Alexander III.

Vladimir Ulyanov in 1887, the year of the execution of his brother Alexander (Sasha), wearing the uniform of the Simbirsk gymnasium (high school).

The origin of this saying goes back to an anecdote told by Lenin's younger sister Maria at his funeral in 1924. According to Maria, when the seventeen-year-old Vladimir heard the news about his older brother's unsuccessful attempt at terror, he said through clenched teeth, 'No, we won't go that way – that's not the way we must go.' Historians have been extremely sceptical about whether Lenin said any such thing, and with good reason. Among the difficulties, Maria herself was only nine years old at the time. Up to this time Vladimir had been concentrating on his studies and was hardly interested in politics, much less endowed with a determined revolutionary outlook. Yet as a summary of the next crucial seven years in Lenin's life, Maria's little anecdote is very insightful.

Picking up where his brother left off and trying to find a new way forward is exactly what Lenin did during these years.

Up to 1886 his brother Alexander had been a typical Ulyanov: an extremely gifted student with a brilliant future ahead of him. He had a particular passion for studying worms and was already winning prizes for his research. Yet in the last months of 1886 Alexander threw himself body and soul into a terrorist organization intent on killing the tsar. He tore himself away from his worms, sold the gold watch he received for his research and used the money to finance the preparation of a homemade bomb. After installing himself in a nearby cottage of a friend in a suburb of St Petersburg, he worked away at the dangerous task of making dynamite out of nitroglycerine. Alexander also penned what he hoped would be verbal dynamite – the manifesto of a group that called itself the Terrorist Faction of the revolutionary organization that assassinated Alexander II in 1881, *Narodnaya volya*. This name can be translated 'People's Will' or 'People's Freedom'. Despite the name, Alexander Ulyanov's group did not have any formal connection with the remnants of the original *Narodnaya volya.*

The underlying cause of the desperation of Alexander and his fellow students was the same fearful official attitude that had contributed to Ilya Ulyanov's death the year before. The tsarist government was unable to forego either educating students or treating them with extreme suspicion. These contradictions were made manifest by a student demonstration in November 1886 to honour the memory of Nikolai Dobroliubov, a radical literary critic of the 1860s. The authorities refused to allow the large crowd of students to go in a body to the cemetery and lay wreaths on his tomb or – even more worrisome from the authorities' point of view – to make speeches. When about 500 students then tried to hold an assembly in a public square they were all detained and questioned for hours by the police chief in person. About forty were arrested and exiled to their provincial homes. This is how the government treated what was supposed to be society's future elite.

The idea of assassinating the new tsar and other high officials was not the brainchild of one small group of radicals. It was in the air, and many student groups, in St Petersburg and elsewhere, converged on this response to their frustrating situation. The plot of Sasha Ulyanov and his friends got further than might be expected. In late February, bomb in hand, one of the plotters walked through the crowded St Petersburg streets, waiting for the signal (a handkerchief raised to the nose) that the tsar was approaching. The tsar didn't come that day. The police picked up some of the plotters for suspicious behaviour on 1 March and only when they were in custody did the police realize that they were carrying bombs. Since the tsar's father had been assassinated on 1 March 1881, the 1887 plot became known as 'the second first of March'.

All members of the conspiracy were quickly rounded up, and the Ulyanov family in Simbirsk received the devastating news that the pride of the family was a would-be regicide. Alexander's mother hurried to Petersburg, was allowed to visit her son, and prevailed on him to make a perfunctory and predictably unsuccessful plea for clemency. On 8 May he and four others were hanged. The outcome of the assassination attempt was not a frightened government making concessions, as the conspirators had hoped, but further regimentation of student life.[5]

What was the thinking that led these young people to attempt murder in order to save Russia, throwing away their own lives in the process? In the manifesto he drafted for his group, Sasha Ulyanov gave the following explanation:

Without freedom of speech, propaganda that is in any way effective is impossible, just as there is no real possibility of improving the economy of the people without the participation of the people's representatives in the administration of the

Alexander (Sasha) Ulyanov, photographed in prison in 1887 while awaiting execution.

country. Thus for Russian socialists the struggle for free institutions is a necessary means for attaining their final aims. . . . Therefore a party that is essentially socialist can only temporarily devote part of its forces to political struggle, insofar as it sees in that struggle a necessary means for making more correct and productive the activity devoted to their final economic ideals.[6]

This passage tells us that Ulyanov's goal was 'free institutions', that is, replacing tsarist absolutism with a constitutional regime and guaranteed political freedoms. But this passage also reveals a certain ambivalence about a merely 'political struggle'. Ulyanov rather apologetically explains why a good socialist, someone whose primary goal is *economic* liberation, must 'temporarily' devote energy to goals espoused by the despised liberals.

Even this grudging acceptance of political struggle (= 'the struggle for free institutions') was the result of a hard-fought internal evolution of Russian socialist radicalism. In the 1860s and 1870s the first wave of Russian socialist revolutionaries saw little that was attractive about political freedom. Such things as freedom of the press were an irrelevant luxury for the largely illiterate peasantry. Indeed, political freedom was actively harmful, serving only to consolidate the rule of the up-and-coming bourgeoisie and to befuddle the masses. The Russian revolutionaries pointed to the eloquent writings of the learned German socialist Karl Marx, who showed just how devastating capitalism could be. Why do anything that would expedite the triumph of this disastrous system?

It followed that the coming Russian revolution could not aim at installing liberal checks and guarantees, thus handing over power to an unpleasant new elite. As the prominent Russian revolutionary Pëtr Lavrov explained, a truly *social* revolution would 'overthrow at once the economic foundations of the present social order'.[7] Perhaps the peasantry's communal traditions endowed it with socialist instincts that would ensure an immediate transition to socialism, as Mikhail Bakunin argued. Or, if not, perhaps a determined minority could seize power and then use an undemocratic state to mould the peasantry – the 'Jacobin' solution of Pëtr Tkachev.

But these dreams of immediate socialist revolution were crushed by the problem pointed out by Sasha Ulyanov in his manifesto: 'Without freedom of speech, propaganda that is in any way effective is impossible.' By the end of the 1870s frustrating failures in making contact with the *narod* had persuaded many of the revolutionaries that the uncongenial task of a merely political revolution really was part of their job description. Perhaps paradoxically, the new interim goal of political freedom was the reason that the revolutionaries turned to terror as a method. Since the current lack of political freedom meant that a mass movement was not yet possible, the only way forward was for a 'handful of daring people' (the self-description of the terrorists) to force the autocratic government to make the necessary concessions. This new strategy upset many revolutionaries (including the future Marxist leader Georgy Plekhanov), not so much because of terror as a method as because of political freedom even as an interim goal.

In 1881 this new strategy led to the first 'first of March': the assassination of Alexander II by *Narodnaya volya*. But even this second wave of Russian socialist radicalism clung to hopes of using the political revolution as a launching pad for *immediate* socialism. They still could not resign themselves to the long-term existence of bourgeois economic and political institutions. As a result, they still had no plausible strategy for using political freedom, once attained, in the cause of socialist revolution.

Many socialists in Western Europe shared the distrust and disdain for 'bourgeois' political freedoms exhibited by their Russian comrades. One prominent strand of European socialism, however, did have a long-term strategy for using political freedom in the cause of socialist revolution. This was Social Democracy, a movement that seemed to combine a mass base with genuine revolutionary fervour (and so the connotations of 'Social Democracy' during this period were almost the opposite of what the term means today). The Social Democratic strategy was inspired by Marx's teaching that the working class as a whole had a world-historical mission to win political power in order to introduce socialism. If working-class rule was the only way to get to socialism, then (as Marx put it, writing in English) the job of the socialists was to make sure that the workers were 'united by combination and led by knowledge' – that is, to help the workers organize and to imbue them with socialist ideology.[8]

This project would only be successful if undertaken on at least a national scale. The implications of Marx's approach were described by a perceptive non-socialist English scholar, John Rae, in 1884, the year after Marx's death:

> The socialists ought to make use of all the abundant means of popular agitation and intercommunication which modern society allowed. No more secret societies in holes and corners, no more small risings and petty plots, but a great broad organization working in open day, and working restlessly by tongue and pen to stir the masses of all European countries to a common international revolution.[9]

This strategy was implied by Marx's whole outlook, but it took on institutional flesh only through the determined efforts of more than one generation of activists, starting with Ferdinand Lassalle in the 1860s and continuing with German party leaders such as Wilhelm Liebknecht and August Bebel, along with unnumbered and anonymous agitators and propagandists. In this way was built the mighty German Social Democratic party (*Sozialdemokratische Partei Deutschlands* or SPD), a source of inspiration for socialists around the world.

Alexander Ulyanov represented a third stage in the internal evolution of Russian socialist radicalism: overthrow the tsar in order to be able to adopt the Social Democratic strategy of 'a great broad organization working in open day, and working restlessly by tongue and pen'. Nevertheless, Alexander considered it obvious that the Social Democratic strategy could only be adopted in the future, *after* political freedom had been won. For the present, terror still seemed to be the only possible method of obtaining political freedom in the absence of political freedom. The use of terror, claimed Ulyanov, was forced on 'an intelligentsia that has been deprived of any possibility of peaceful, cultural influence on social life'. Under the present repressive circumstances, the workers could do no more than provide support for a preliminary political revolution that would be led by the terror-wielding intelligentsia.

This reasoning led Alexander to throw away his life with no result other than a hardening of government repression. Russian socialist radicalism had arrived at a dead end. The Social Democratic strategy of educating workers by mass campaigns was perceived as the only realistic way to get to socialism, but it could not be applied without political freedom – and there seemed to be no way to obtain the requisite political freedom. The Social Democratic strategy itself was inapplicable under tsarist absolutism, while terrorism had been tried and found wanting. This was the strategic dilemma facing Russian socialist radicalism, and it was presented to Vladimir Ulyanov in the most devastatingly personal terms.

Vladimir's search in the years following his brother's execution led him to the conclusion that a stripped-down, bare-bones version of the Social Democratic strategy could be applied *even under tsarism* as a way of obtaining the political freedom required for a full and unadulterated application of the same strategy. But, as we shall see, Vladimir's 'other way' to achieving his brother's goal was based on a heroic scenario shot through with optimistic assumptions about the inspiring power of class leadership.

Lenin never mentioned his brother in public. Nevertheless, he often invoked the Russian revolutionary tradition as a whole and pictured himself as fulfilling its long-held aims. In 1920, addressing himself to newly-minted communists from around the world, he said that the Russian revolutionary tradition had 'suffered its way' to Marxism.[10] He meant the evolution that I have just described, in which the frustrations and martyrdom of people like Alexander Ulyanov led ultimately to the rise of Russian Social Democracy. Lenin's emotional investment in his heroic scenario arose in large part from his hope that it would make all these sacrifices meaningful.

Marxism shows Lenin 'Another Way'

The first stage in Lenin's groping toward 'another way' was straight-forward student protest against government over-regimentation of university life. After passing his final gymnasium exams in spring 1887 with his usual high marks, Vladimir entered Kazan University in the autumn of that year to study law. There he got immediately into student politics and came to the notice of the authorities when he was involved in a disruptive student demonstration. Since the authorities had to submit reports on all participants, we have a verbal snapshot of perhaps Vladimir's first attempt at leadership: '[On 4 December, V. Ulyanov] threw himself into the first assembly hall and he and Poliansky were the first to dash along the corridor of the second floor, shouting and waving their hands, as if to inspire the others. After leaving the student meeting, he handed in his student card.'[11]

Kicked out of university, Lenin was sent to live under police observance in the nearby village of Kokushkino. Lenin later complained to Krupskaya about the way polite society dropped his family after Alexander's execution. This social rejection should not obscure the support and sympathy that polite 'liberal' society gave the students expelled from university, loading them with gifts as they left. In fact, over the years, the Ulyanovs certainly benefited from their connection with Alexander and the prestige that this connection gave them in the eyes of a public opinion that was extremely hostile to tsarism.

Lenin later recalled that the following summer in the village of Kokushkino was the most intensive bout of reading of his entire life. His reading pushed him to the next stage of his evolution as he discovered the Russian revolutionary tradition. The author who had the most influence on him was Nikolai Chernyshevsky, an outstanding radical journalist and scholar of the 1860s. Cherny-shevsky had been in Siberian exile since 1864 and had one year to

Lenin during his student days in Samara.

live when Lenin read his works in 1888. Lenin found out his address and sent him a letter, although he never got a reply. Lenin learned many things from Chernyshevsky, but perhaps the real legacy of the older writer to Lenin was a visceral hatred of philistinism. Lenin felt that Chernyshevsky had a 'pitch-perfect' sense of what was truly revolutionary and what was 'philistine' compromise and conformism.

In October 1888 restrictions were loosened enough to allow Vladimir and his family to move back to Kazan. Here the properly Marxist stage of Vladimir's evolution began, as he participated in illegal Social Democratic reading circles and began to cut his teeth on Marx's *Capital*. Here began the love affair with the writings of Marx and Engels that continued all his life.

In 1889 the Ulyanovs moved to the Volga city of Samara, where for the next few years Vladimir continued his Marxist self-education and began to work out his own Marxist interpretation of Russian reality. Lenin's Marxist reading of the vast social changes going on in Russia provided him with the basis of his heroic scenario of class leadership and, in so doing, pointed to the 'other way' his brother had failed to find. Vladimir could now be confident that 'the force was with him' – the force of History, with a capital H.

The dilemma facing Alexander Ulyanov and the Russian revolutionary tradition as a whole was that political freedom was necessary in order to prepare for a socialist revolution based on the masses, but political freedom itself was impossible to achieve without a mass movement. But what if a mighty, irresistible force was even now at work, vastly increasing the *potential* for a mass movement despite tsarist repression? If so, even a relatively feeble and persecuted Social Democratic party could have a tremendous effect, if a way could be found to tap into this vast potential.

Looking through his Marxist spectacles, Lenin perceived such a mighty force: the capitalist transformation of Russia. In the long run, of course, capitalist transformation would lay the necessary groundwork for a successful socialist revolution. But socialist revolution was not Lenin's most urgent problem. He was much more interested in possible mass support for the preceding democratic and anti-tsarist revolution that would install political freedom. What Lenin perceived behind the dry statistical tables of land ownership and employment was the creation of new fighters who were both willing and able to wrest political freedom from the grip of the absolutist tsarist government. These fighters consisted of the new classes created by capitalist transformation out of the old Russian *narod*. There were several such classes, each with its particular role to play in Lenin's heroic scenario.

The first of these new classes was the urban factory workers. The urban workers' assigned role in Lenin's scenario was to be 'the sole and natural representative of Russia's entire labouring and exploited population and [therefore] capable of raising the banner of worker emancipation'. The factory workers were the natural leaders of the *narod* because they directly faced in pure form the same thing (Lenin was convinced) that confronted all Russia's labourers, since 'the exploitation of the working people in Russia *is everywhere capitalist in nature*'. But while capitalist exploitation provided a link with the *narod* in the countryside, the urban environment gave the factory workers special leadership qualities. Their concentration in towns and in large-scale factories made them easier to organize. Even more important, they were in a position to read and heed the Marxist message about the causes of and the remedy for capitalist exploitation. In contrast, in the countryside, 'exploitation is still enmeshed in medieval forms, various political, legal and conventional trappings, tricks and devices, which hinder the working people and their ideologists from seeing the essence of the system which oppresses the working people, from seeing where and how a way can be found out of this system.'[12]

The second class created by capitalist transformation was the exploited workers who remained in the countryside. Lenin's heroic scenario depended crucially on the argument that capitalist exploitation was ubiquitous, not only in the cities, but in villages and farms all over Russia. These rural workers may not have been able to play the role of class leaders, but they could step into the essential role of class *followers*. Capitalism was shaking them up, pushing them out of their villages and into a brave new world. And when such a worker 'leaves home to tramp the whole of Russia' and 'hires himself out now to a landlord, tomorrow to a railway contractor', he will see many things not previously visible. He will see that

> wherever he goes he is most shamefully plundered; that other
> paupers like himself are plundered; that it is not necessarily

the 'lord' who robs him, but also 'his brother muzhik' [fellow peasant], if the latter has the money to buy labour-power; that the government will always serve the bosses, restrict the rights of the workers and suppress every attempt to protect their most elementary rights, calling these attempts rebellious riots.[13]

This newly visible rightlessness gives the village poor a stake in a *political* revolution. The *narod*, Lenin insisted, was even now breaking up into two opposed classes: workers on one side and a new bourgeoisie of peasant origin on the other. Ultimately, these two new classes would be bitter enemies. Social Democracy could therefore not undertake to organize or lead peasant farmers. Nevertheless, the emerging peasant bourgeoisie was yet another mass force in support of a political revolution. As opposed to elite factory owners, who resented tsarism but could always cut a deal with the authorities, the new bourgeoisie of the *narod*, the peasant farmers, were willing to fight and fight hard to rid the country of the coercive 'survivals of serfdom' and, in particular, the social and economic privileges of the landed estate-owners.

Capitalist transformation was thus creating new mass fighters with a stake in a successful political revolution. Foremost among these were the workers in both town and country – even though the political revolution would *strengthen* bourgeois rule in the short run. Nevertheless, the exploited workers have a life-and-death interest, not only in the far-distant *socialist* revolution that will end capitalism, but also in the here-and-now *democratic* revolution for political freedom that will make capitalism less intolerable. As a good Marxist, Lenin is supposed to denounce capitalist exploitation and he duly does. But these condemnations get somewhat lost in the shuffle, because Lenin is more vitally concerned with showing that there are worse things than capitalist exploitation. The kind of pre-capitalist exploitation still prevalent in Russia was worse, because it relied on coercion, personal dependence, lack of mobility and isolation. Worst of all is capitalist exploitation that was intensified by coercive survivals of the pre-capitalist order – first and foremost by tsarism itself.

Capitalism was therefore 'progressive', and not only because it was creating new classes that were both willing and able to fight in a nationwide struggle against tsarism. It was also shattering 'age-old immobility and routine, destroying the settled life of the peasants who vegetated behind their medieval partitions, and creating new social classes striving of necessity towards contact, unification, and active participation in the whole of the economic (and not only economic) life of the country and the whole world'.[14] Lenin's seemingly offhand parenthetical comment – 'and not only economic' – reveals the connection between his learned Marxist analysis and his passionate heroic scenario. The new classes are also called upon to participate in the *political* life of the country, indeed, to revolutionize it.

In the early 1890s, as Lenin was working out his life-long political identity, he also had to fight against another view of Marx's implications for Russian revolutionary strategy. This view was put forth by the bitterest opponents of the Russian Marxists, namely, the older generation of *narodniki* or populists who were appalled at the infatuation with Marxism displayed by a younger generation of socialist radicals. For veterans of revolutionary struggles, such as Nikolai Mikhailovsky, the Marxist strategy was grotesquely long-term, passive and callous about the fate of the Russian peasant. According to these hostile witnesses Russian Marxists had written off the peasantry. In fact (in Mikhailovsky's words) they 'directly insist on the further devastation of the village'.[15] Capitalism (cheered on by the Marxists) would force the crushed and impoverished peasants to migrate to the cities, become factory workers and (after a generation or two of capitalist hell) carry out the socialist revolution.

One of Mikhailovsky's colleagues, S. N. Krivenko, sharpened the portrait by arguing that simple consistency required Russian

Marxists to actively encourage capitalist production, speculate in peasant land and rejoice as peasants were kicked off the land.[16] One quip of his was especially successful. Krivenko suggested that if the Marxists thought capitalism was so great, they should open up village taverns to speed it along. One Russian Social Democrat later recalled that, as a young student in St Petersburg in the early 1890s, his fellow students would slap him on the back and say, 'Hey, Marxist, when are you opening a tavern?'[17]

Lenin was still in Samara in 1891 when a massive famine hit the Volga region and elsewhere. The famine first horrified and then enraged Russian society as it observed what was widely felt to be the evasion and later the bungling and outright corruption of the official response. According to one memoir account, Vladimir Ulyanov reacted to the famine exactly as predicted by Mikhailovsky and Krivenko. Vasily Vodovozov was on good terms with the Ulyanov family in Samara in the early 1890s. In his memoir, written in the 1920s, he tells us that Vladimir Ulyanov 'sharply and definitely spoke out against feeding the hungry'. The young Marxist insisted that the famine was 'a progressive factor. By destroying the peasant economy and throwing the *muzhik* out of the village into the town, the famine would create a proletariat and aid the industrialization of the region.' Furthermore, the famine 'will force the *muzhik* to think about the foundations of the capitalist system'.[18] Young Ulyanov is thus a sort of Marxist Scrooge: Are there no prisons? And the Union workhouses – are they still in operation? And if people would rather die than go there, they had better do it and decrease the surplus population.

Vodovozov's story is neat, too neat, as a hard-boiled detective might say. The young Lenin becomes a walking, talking embodiment of the most hostile stereotypes of Russian Marxism circulating at the time. Many historians still today believe in the accuracy of this polemical caricature of Russian Marxism in general and Lenin in particular. But Lenin's actual vision of the 'other way' created by capitalism was far otherwise. He saw capitalist transformation of the Russian countryside as the objective force that made the heroic scenario of inspirational class leadership possible in the here and now.

According to the hostile stereotype, the Russian Marxists called on capitalism to *crush* the peasants, drive them *out* of the countryside and into the cities, and thus prepare the way for a long-distant *socialist* revolution. In reality, Lenin gave capitalism the mission of *transforming* the peasants, making them effective fighters while still *in* the countryside, and thus making possible a *democratic* revolution based on the masses and not on the isolated and therefore terror-wielding intelligentsia.

Given his actual scenario, Lenin reacted to the caricature of the Marxist Scrooge with indignant rage. In *Friends of the People*, he cited the comments by Mikhailovsky and Krivenko quoted earlier and responded: suppose Mikhailovsky did meet someone in some literary salon who spouted this nonsense and passed it off as Marxism. Poseurs like this 'besmirched the banner' of Russian Social Democracy. To tell the reading public that this repulsive caricature was an accurate portrayal of Russian Marxism was nothing but the most blatant *poshlost* or philistinism.[19]

As the Marxist Scrooge, Lenin is supposed to have actively willed the peasants' situation to be as bad as possible. But in 1899 he wrote that 'Social Democrats cannot remain indifferent spectators of the starvation of the peasants and their destruction from death by starvation. Never could there be two opinions among Russian Social Democrats about the necessity of the broadest possible help to the starving peasants.' An otherwise hostile émigré memoirist remembers Lenin himself working in one of the canteens set up to help the peasants in 1891–2.[20]

Lenin's Marxist analysis of the development of Russian capitalism undergirded his heroic scenario by proving three things: the proletariat has been given the role of leader; 'the strength of the proletariat in the process of history is immeasurably greater than its share of the total population'; the deep-rooted remnants of serfdom give rise to the profound revolutionary drive of the peasantry.[21] Lenin's Marx-based heroic scenario helps to explain why he literally fell in love with Marx's writings. We can imagine Vladimir addressing the ghost of his martyred brother in words such as these: No, Sasha, we will not get to political freedom by throwing away our lives in futile attempts to frighten the government into concessions. There is another way: an epic national struggle in which the urban workers will lead the newly galvanized *narod*. This will work, Sasha! It is guaranteed by the authority of the greatest socialist of all, Karl Marx.

Lenin Becomes a Revolutionary Social Democrat

His Marxist studies did not distract Lenin from obtaining professional credentials as a lawyer. He managed to obtain permission to take external exams at Petersburg University and in April 1891 he travelled to St Petersburg for that purpose. For the rest of the year he had to answer questions on topics as diverse as Plato's dialogue *The Laws*, Roman law and the degrees of 'unfreedom' among the peasants of feudal Russia. Despite another family tragedy – his twenty-year-old sister Olga, who was living in St Petersburg, died of typhoid fever on 8 May 1891 – he aced the examination and duly received certification as a lawyer.

Returning to Samara, he could now earn something like a living by defending local peasants on charges typically involving petty theft. But the big city beckoned, and in August 1893 he ended the Volga chapter of his life by moving to St Petersburg. Upon arriving, he dutifully wrote a letter to his mother, telling her that he had found a room that was clear and light, in a building that had a good entrance and was 'only some fifteen minutes walk from the library'

Four-year-old Vladimir with his younger sister, Olga, Simbirsk, 1874.

(a primary consideration for Lenin everywhere he lived). After asking for money to tide him over, he confessed that 'obviously I have not been living carefully; in one month I have spent a rouble and thirty-six kopecks on the horse trams, for instance. When I get used to the place I shall probably spend less.'[22] Lenin used his various contacts to establish himself immediately. He got a position with the lawyer M. F. Volkenstein. Much more important to him, he used letters of introduction in order to join a Marxist circle at the Technology Institute, through which he was able to get in touch with worker study groups. He had found the milieu in which he would spend the rest of his life.

Lenin had already worked out the Marxist underpinnings of his heroic scenario. He had, to his own satisfaction, demonstrated the objective *potential* for applying a Social Democratic strategy to Russia: an underground party inspires urban factory workers with a sense of their historical mission to lead the *narod* against tsarism. In St Petersburg in 1893–4 he found reason enough to decide that actual Russian activists and actual Russian workers could work together to realize this potential. Some of these reasons came from developments in international Social Democracy. Among these was the resounding triumph of German Social Democracy during its own 'outlaw period'. The German Chancellor, Otto Bismarck, had tried to destroy Social Democracy with repressive legislation in 1878 – and lo and behold, by 1891 Bismarck was gone but the German Social Democratic party was still there. Indeed, it seemed as if Bismarck's anti-socialist laws had made the party stronger. The anti-socialist laws were allowed to lapse, the party held a triumphant congress in the German town of Erfurt at the end of 1891, and a new party programme was adopted that became a model for Social Democrats everywhere. Perhaps Social Democracy *could* thrive even when subjected to energetic state repression.

The overwhelming influence of the German party on international Social Democracy was further increased by the *Erfurt Programme* (1892), a book-length explication of the Social Democratic strategy written by the up-and-coming Marxist writer Karl Kautsky. Kautsky was born into a Czech family in 1854 and came to Social Democracy only after a period as a Czech nationalist. He served for a term in the Austrian Social Democratic party and then moved to Germany to become the editor of the theoretical journal *Die Neue Zeit* (New Times), a post he retained until the First World War. His influence on Russian Social Democracy and Lenin personally was incalculable, and we shall meet him again in every chapter of this book.

In many ways Kautsky's book was unoriginal popularization. But a clear exposition of basic principles, an inspiring application to the contemporary situation and a compelling overarching narrative can have a profound impact on events, whether it is original or not. More importantly for Lenin personally, Kautsky's version of Social Democracy also contained a heroic scenario of class leadership – one that, like Lenin's, assigned the workers a national mission. In the *Erfurt Programme* Kautsky wrote that Social Democracy has a tendency to become more and more 'a *Volkspartei*, in the sense that it is the representative not only of the industrial wage-labourers but of all the labouring and exploited strata – and therefore the great majority of the population, what is commonly known as "the *Volk*"' (= *narod* in Russian).[23]

Kautsky also emphasized that Social Democrats had a duty, not only to use political freedoms, but to struggle to win them where they were absent. Political freedoms were 'light and air for the proletariat; he who lets them wither or withholds them – he who keeps the proletariat from the struggle to win these freedoms and to extend them – that person is one of the proletariat's worst enemies.'[24] In short, Lenin could feel that his own heroic scenario had received the authoritative endorsement of one of Europe's leading Marxists. No wonder Lenin took the trouble to translate the *Erfurt Programme* into Russian during the summer of 1894.

As we saw in the Introduction, Lenin's widow Nadezhda Krupskaya identified St Petersburg as the time and place where Lenin acquired his heroic scenario – his confidence that 'all the labouring masses, all the oppressed' will follow the industrial working class and thus assure its victory. According to Krupskaya the final push for this life-defining commitment was Lenin's 'work among the workers of Piter [St Petersburg], conversations with these workers, attentive listening to their speeches'.

Was Krupskaya suggesting that these workers were committed Marxists who lectured Lenin on the fine points of theory? Not at all. When Lenin moved to St Petersburg and had regular contact for the first time with real workers, he did not learn that the workers

'A Type of Russian Working Man', an illustration from William Walling's *Russia's Message* (1908).

were necessarily wonderful and noble people. What he learned was that some of them were fighters who were willing to have conversations with intellectuals like himself. He became convinced that they could indeed play the role assigned to them by the Social Democratic scenario. Lenin also discovered the rudiments of a specifically Social Democratic underground, that is, a set of institutions that allowed Social Democratic activists to have ongoing contact with militant workers.

In Lenin's view Social Democracy represented not rejection of but rather connection with the earlier Russian revolutionary tradition. The Social Democratic strategy was what the Russian revolutionaries had been groping toward, through heroic mistakes and suffering. It was the answer to the problem that his older brother had tried, and failed, to solve. As we shall see in the next chapter much hard work by a whole generation of Social Democratic activists, many ups and downs, many internal controversies, were needed to make his life-defining wager on his heroic scenario begin to pay off.

Lenin announced his new political identity to the world in the first half of 1894 by writing a book of several hundred pages entitled *Who are These 'Friends of the People' and How Do They Fight Against the Social Democrats?*. In what turned out to be very typical fashion, Lenin's exposition of his vision of Russian Social Democracy came in the form of an angry polemic against the 'philistines' who attacked it. The phrase 'friends of the people' was a self-description of Russian populists such as Mikhailovsky, used ironically by Lenin. *Friends of the People* was Lenin's first publication, albeit an illegal one. For a long time, all copies of it were presumed missing. When two-thirds of it showed up in 1923 Lenin's companions and first biographers – Grigory Zinoviev, Lev Kamenev and Krupskaya – were thrilled. They saw *Friends of the People* as proof that right at the start of his career Lenin had acquired the essentials of the world-view that guided him for the rest of his life – and they were right.

Lenin Unfurls his Banner

The banners that were unfurled in the street demonstrations by Social Democratic workers both in Russia and Europe became a central icon of the socialist movement. To appear in public under a banner with a revolutionary slogan was the essential militant act. The image of the banner was an extremely important one for Lenin himself. It was more than just a figure of speech found littered throughout his writings – it was a metaphor that focused his conception of revolutionary politics. The banner announced to the world who you were and what you were fighting for. The implied narrative summarized in the slogans on the banner inspired your own fighters and rallied others to the cause. The banner signified the moral unity of the fighters that made possible their effective organization. Like the flag for a patriotic citizen, the waving banner with its militant message summed up all the emotional warmth that gave life to the dry bones of Marxist theory.

By 1894 Lenin had worked out the heroic scenario which informed his entire political career. He summed up this scenario in the last sentence of *Friends of the People*. The original edition (illegally published by the primitive hectograph method) shows the prominence accorded to these final words. When *Friends of the People* was rediscovered in the 1920s Lenin's long-time comrade Grigorii Zinoviev was particularly taken with Lenin's final sentence: 'These words, written almost thirty years ago, sound as if they had been written today.'[25] Indeed, Lenin's long and carefully crafted sentence unfurled the banner under which he was to march for the rest of his life:

> When the advanced representatives of this class assimilate the ideas of scientific socialism and the idea of the historical role of the Russian worker – when these ideas receive a broad dissemination – when durable organisations are created among the workers that transform the present uncoordinated economic war of the workers into a purposive class struggle, – then the Russian WORKER, elevated to the head of all democratic elements, will overthrow absolutism and lead the RUSSIAN PROLETARIAT (side by side with the proletariat of ALL COUNTRIES) by the *direct road of open political struggle to* THE VICTORIOUS COMMUNIST REVOLUTION.[26]

Lenin's sentence sketches out a world-historical drama starting in Russia in the 1890s and ending with the victorious communist

The Angel of Socialism in the Russian copy of Walter Crane's *The Capitalist Vampire.*

revolution. This drama can be divided into three acts, with each act unified by a single task that has to be accomplished before the curtain rises for the next act. Remarkably enough, Lenin lived to see this entire drama played out, albeit accompanied with the shortfalls, ironies and frustrations that life usually hands out. Each decade of his thirty-year revolutionary career corresponds to one act of the drama – and one chapter of this book (the tumultuous final decade gets two chapters).

Act One, The Creation of Russian Social Democracy: '*When the advanced representatives of this class assimilate the ideas of scientific socialism, the idea of the historical role of the Russian worker – when these ideas receive a broad dissemination – when durable organisations are created among the workers that transform the present uncoordinated economic war of the workers into a purposive class struggle . . .*'

Act One tells the story of the creation of a Russian version of a Social Democratic party that is genuinely and effectively engaged in bringing what Marx called 'knowledge and combination' to the workers, despite being forced underground by tsarist repression. For Lenin, this act of the drama took place during the years 1894–1904.

The emotional content of Act One can be seen in Walter Crane's poster of the Angel of Socialism. This poster was originally published in England in 1885, but Russianized (with the artist's consent) in 1902 by Russian émigrés living in London – just as Lenin's Act One is a Russian version of a process that (as Kautsky and others taught him) had already taken place in other countries. Instead of the original text of 'Religious Hypocrisy, Capitalism, Party Politics', the wings of the vampire bat in the Russian version say: 'Bureaucracy, Church, Capital, Autocracy'. The bat is gnawing the vitals of the sleeping worker (identified as 'labour') who is unaware of what is happening. An angel blows a trumpet to open his eyes and to invite him to fight back under a banner that reads 'socialism'. International Social Democracy saw itself in no less exalted terms. Its mission was to imbue the workers with a sense of their own mission.

Act Two, The Democratic Revolution: '*then the Russian worker, elevated to the head of all democratic elements, will overthrow absolutism . . .*'

Act Two presents the struggle to bring political freedom to Russia by revolutionary overthrow of the tsar. This struggle was Lenin's central concern in the years 1904 to 1914. Bolshevism emerged in Russia during this decade as a distinct current within Social Democracy, defined by a specific strategy for bringing political freedom to Russia – a strategy based squarely on Lenin's heroic scenario of the working class leading the *narod*. In Lenin's banner sentence the *narod* is given the label 'democratic elements'. This bit of Marxist jargon means all those who want an anti-tsarism

Walter Crane's illustration of the Russian liberation struggle.

revolution enough to really fight for it. In Lenin's mind the main 'democratic elements' were the urban workers and the *narod*.

The emotional meaning of this episode is shown in a later poster by Walter Crane, created specifically at the request of Russian Social Democrats in London – just as Lenin's Act Two concerns a specifically Russian task not faced by Social Democracy in Europe. In contrast to the worker in the previous poster, the central figure here has awakened and filed through the chains that kept him from acting. He looks with grim determination at the crowned eagle of tsarism that has dug its claws into him. The worker has unfurled his banner: 'Down with Autocracy! Long live Freedom and Socialism!' The eagle is taken aback, but obviously the struggle will be difficult. In the background a crowd of militant workers and peasants (is that a hammer or an axe that is being held aloft?), under streaming banners, are moving toward the fight.

A Soviet poster from 1920 celebrating the third anniversary of the October Revolution.

Act Three, The Social Revolution: The Russian worker will 'lead the RUSSIAN PROLETARIAT (side by side with the proletariat of ALL COUNTRIES) by the direct road of open political struggle to THE VICTORIOUS COMMUNIST REVOLUTION.'

Act Three in Lenin's heroic scenario is the world socialist revolution. During the final decade of Lenin's career, 1914 to 1924, his central concern was carrying out the socialist revolution both at home in Russia and in Western Europe. When war broke out in 1914 and the various Social Democratic parties renounced international solidarity and participated in national defence, Lenin felt that 'the banner of Social Democracy has been besmirched' and began to insist on a name change from Social Democrat to Communist. In this final act Lenin no longer defined himself primarily as a Russian Social Democrat but as a leader of the world communist movement. Yet, even as a Communist, Lenin remained loyal to his 1894 scenario.

The emotional content of this act is revealed by a Soviet poster from 1920. The Russian worker, still with his anachronistic blacksmith's hammer, stands amid the ruins of tsarism's once mighty edifice. The crown that was once atop the eagle's head is now lying disregarded in the rubble. Yet the banner unfurled by the Russian worker makes a prouder claim than simply to have achieved political freedom and the possibility of 'open political struggle'. It displays (unfortunately not visible here) the initials of an actual revolutionary regime, the Russian Soviet Federated Socialist Republic. Inspired by his example are many workers who stand under their own banners with the slogan 'Workers of the world, unite!' in various languages.

By 1894 Ulyanov had adopted the public identity later known as 'N. Lenin'. The particular pseudonym 'Lenin' was first used only in 1901 but Vladimir Ulyanov had already defined himself as an activist of the Social Democratic underground by 1894. More importantly, he had found the 'other way' that would allow him to stride forward with the uncanny self-confidence that so bemused observers. The sentence that concluded *Friends of the People* was a banner, not unlike the banner carried by the angel of socialism, the banner of the awakened Russian worker, the banner of the European proletariat on the march. The dramatic and ambitious narrative on that banner was Lenin's story – and he stuck to it.

2

The Merger of Socialism and the Worker Movement

Boris Gorev was one of the young Social Democratic activists with whom Lenin teamed up after he arrived in St Petersburg in 1893. Gorev later remembered coming home one day during the great Petersburg strikes of 1895–6 and finding two of his women friends – fellow activists in the nascent Social Democratic underground – twirling around the apartment in sheer delight.[1]

What exhilarated these young people, in spite of the long and dangerous hours they were putting in to support the striking workers? As we shall see, the imposing dimensions of the strike not only showed the potential for a militant worker movement in Russia – more fundamentally, the strike validated the wager these young activists had made about the workability of the Social Democratic strategy in tsarist Russia. Lenin had made the same wager in as public a manner as underground conditions permitted in his underground manifesto *Friends of the People*. Lenin may not have danced around his apartment (or he may have!), but his writings during the 1890s reveal the same sense of excited pride.

Lenin in St Petersburg, 1894–6

To understand this exhilarating sense of confirmation, we need to know what Lenin was doing during his two years in Petersburg, the meaning he gave to his own activities and the ways in which

From a revolutionary magazine of the 1905–7 era. Its caption read: 'The working man who reads indulges in a dangerous occupation'.

the Petersburg strikes of the mid-1890s validated this meaning. In all of this Lenin was a typical Social Democratic activist – or, rather, he was exceptional only in the fervour and energy with which he threw himself into his new role.

When Lenin arrived in Petersburg in late 1893 his first aim was to get in touch with existing Social Democratic circles. The most active circle consisted of students at the university's technology institute. The energy and erudition of the newcomer from the Volga quickly made him a leader. Over the next two years Lenin worked with other activists such as L. Martov to bring greater organizational structure to the various Social Democratic groups in the city. These efforts culminated in late 1895 with the creation

Members of the Petersburg Union of Struggle for the Liberation of the Working Class. This photograph was taken in early 1897, after the arrest of the Union's leaders and shortly before their exile to Siberia. Lenin is directly behind the table; seated to his left, with one arm resting on the table, is L. Martov, a later leader of the Mensheviks and Lenin's political enemy.

of the Union of Struggle for the Liberation of the Working Class. The title 'Union of Struggle' soon became the standard one for local Social Democratic organizations.

A great rite of initiation for these young activists was their first contact with the worker groups who requested propagandists from the intelligentsia. In the Social Democratic jargon of the time, the term 'propaganda' had connotations that were very different from those it later acquired. It did not mean simplistic messages used to bombard passive targets, but rather an intensive and wide-ranging education that was initiated by the workers. 'Propagandized worker' was therefore a title of honour, an indication of potential leader status. These propaganda circles gave rise to Lenin's conversations with workers that Krupskaya later claimed were so crucial to his self-definition.

Lenin also collaborated with workers in carrying out investigations of factory conditions in places like the Thornton works in St Petersburg. Later he recounted how one worker, worn out by Lenin's relentless grilling, 'told me with a smile, wiping the sweat away after the end of our labours, "working overtime is not as tough for me as answering your questions!".[2]

As at all periods of his life, literary activities took up much of Lenin's time. Partly these were writings aimed at an intelligentsia audience that was passionately attentive to the debates between the young Marxists and the older writers in the populist tradition. For this audience Lenin produced polemical essays with titles like 'A Line-by-Line Critique of a Populist *Profession de foi*' (the populists or *narodniki* were the dominant current in the Russian revolutionary tradition prior to the rise of Social Democracy).[3] Lenin also wrote directly for the workers, for example, a forty-page pamphlet setting forth the worker's legal position in relation to factory fines. When the émigré Social Democrat Pavel Axelrod praised this pamphlet, Lenin gratefully responded: 'I wanted nothing so much, dreamed of nothing so much, as the possibility of writing for the workers.'[4]

Lenin had met Axelrod during a trip abroad in the summer of 1895. This trip represents one more dimension of Lenin's activities during his time in Petersburg, namely, the effort to establish contacts with the wider Social Democratic world. In Switzerland Lenin met with Axelrod and other members of the Group for the Liberation of Labour such as Georgy Plekhanov and Vera Zasulich. The Group for the Liberation of Labour, one of the earliest Russian Marxist organizations, had been founded about a decade earlier and was now delighted to be able to make contact with a living, breathing Social Democratic movement in Russia. Lenin was also received by one of the legendary leaders of the German Social Democratic party, Wilhelm Liebknecht. Returning home, Lenin supported efforts to make contacts with other Russian towns where similar embryonic Social Democratic groups had arisen.

Lenin's various activities – polemicizing with populists, working with local activists, making contact with factory workers, visits to émigré leaders abroad – were all tied together in his mind as part of the larger story of European Social Democracy. He and his fellow activists were consciously replicating a process they thought had already taken place in other countries. Naturally, Russian conditions imposed crucial variations but, as Lenin saw it, these variations did not alter the underlying logic of what was going on.

The person who set out this underlying logic most effectively was Karl Kautsky in the *Erfurt Programme*, and herein lies the source of Kautsky's huge impact on fledgling Russian Social Democracy. Kautsky's definition of Social Democracy became universally accepted in the international Social Democratic movement: 'Social Democracy is the merger of socialism and the worker movement.' 'Worker movement' in this slogan means a militant, anti-capitalist, self-protection movement of worker protest. 'Socialism' means the socialist message, as spread by committed propagandists and agitators. Social Democracy happens when the two sides realize that they need each other. The worker movement acknowledges that only socialism can truly end worker exploitation and misery. The socialists acknowledge that socialism can only be established when the workers themselves understand its necessity and are ready to fight for it. As Kautsky goes on to explain, the two geniuses who first understood the need for the merger of socialism and the worker movement were Marx and Engels.[5]

According to Kautsky, many barriers of mistrust and misunderstanding had to be overcome before the merger could take place. At first the socialist intellectuals (including intellectuals of worker origin) did not aim their message directly at the oppressed and downtrodden workers themselves. They assumed that the workers, precisely because they were downtrodden, were incapable of understanding the necessity of socialism. In response, the militant workers fighting the battles of their class viewed socialism as nothing more than the hobby-horse of patronizing intellectuals. But (Kautsky fervently believed) this original separation would inevitably be overcome in each country. This pattern was confirmed by 'the history of all countries' (a phrase used by Lenin more than once to make this point) – and so the Russian Social Democrats of the 1890s could take heart that the merger would eventually take place in Russia as well.

Lenin explicitly endorsed Kautsky's merger formula in his seminal *Friends of the People* in 1894. As he put it later, 'Kautsky's expression . . . reproduces the basic ideas of the *Communist Manifesto*'.[6] More than that, the merger formula runs like a red thread through Lenin's writings from 1894 to 1904 whenever Lenin had occasion to state his basic purposes. When asked by his colleagues to write a draft of a Social Democratic programme (even though he was in jail at the time), Lenin wrote that Social Democracy showed 'the way by which the aspiration of socialism – the aspiration of ending the eternal exploitation of man by man – must be merged with the movement of the *narod* that arose out of the conditions of life created by large-scale factories and workshops.'[7]

Lenin used Kautsky's merger formula to give meaning to his various activities, since all were in aid of bringing committed socialists and militant workers into a single fighting organization. And in this Lenin was again typical, since activists all over Russia were similarly inspired. Indeed, Kautsky has as good a title as anyone to be called the father of Russian Social Democracy – or rather, he was the channel by which the 'basic ideas of the *Communist Manifesto*' and the prestige of the German socialist party (SPD) were brought home to the young Russians for whom Kautsky's *Erfurt Programme* became a textbook of Social Democracy.

Lenin and his fellow activists very much wanted to see Russian Social Democracy as one more exemplar of the canonical merger, of course with the necessary changes having been made. The crucial necessary change was adjusting to the absence of political freedom. Tsarist repression meant that both 'socialism' (the activists) and 'the worker movement' (unions, strikes, economic protest) had only a passing resemblance to their counterparts in Western Europe. Could functional Russian equivalents be found to serve the same basic purpose?

On the 'socialism' side, the interaction of Social Democratic ideals with the realities of Russian society lead to the creation of a new social type, the *praktik*, the activists who actually ran local organizations. This new type was something of a hybrid, made up of both plebeian intellectuals and '*intelligentnye* workers' (workers who adopted intelligentsia ideals). The worker contribution to this hybrid social type, crucial both to Social Democratic discourse and practice, was called the 'purposive worker' (more usually translated as 'conscious worker'). The purposive worker was not only militant, but also determined to be 'rational and cultured'. He or she wanted to think well, to behave well, to dress well, to use proper grammar and to avoid strong drink. Semën Kanatchikov, a worker whose memoirs are the best entrée into the outlook of this social type, describes himself:

> Sufficiently fortified by now by my awareness that I was 'adult', 'independent', and, what is more, 'purposive', I bravely entered into combat with 'human injustice'. I stood up for the abused and the oppressed, enlightened and persuaded the 'non-purposive', and argued passionately with my opponents, defending my ideals.[8]

But this sense of mission and self-worth was fragile, and Kanatchikov recalls the loneliness of a 'few solitary revolutionary youths' among 'the inert, sometimes even hostile masses'.[9]

Only a determined optimist could see these young and inexperienced Russian *praktiki* as the functional equivalent of socialist activists in Western European countries. Kautsky's merger scenario also required a working class that was capable of sustained and 'purposive' class struggle. Did the Russian working class – made up of newly arrived peasants thrown without preparation into the factory cauldron – have the necessary cultural level to move from passivity to organized protest, from destructive riots to disciplined strikes? A sceptical Social Democrat, Elena Kuskova, wrote in 1899 that the actual results of capitalist industrialization in Russia were indeed 'depressing and capable of plunging the most optimistic Marxist . . . into gloom'.[10]

These very understandable doubts were the reason that the Petersburg strikes of 1896 were so exhilarating for the Social Democratic *praktiki*. Their impact can best be gauged by remarks made by the liberal historian and party leader Paul Miliukov, writing less than a decade after the event: 'In June, 1896, St Petersburg was roused by a startling movement of workingmen, the like of which it had never before seen. The workers in twenty-two cotton factories of the northern capital, numbering more than thirty thousand, organized something like a general strike.' The demands of the workers were sensible and moderate, the conduct of the strike was disciplined and peaceful. The strike was not instigated by socialists from the intelligentsia, and 'all the proclamations and other papers published during the strike were written by the men themselves, in a plain, half-educated language'.

Thus the 1896 strikes stand in startling contrast to earlier more destructive and anarchic worker outbursts. According to Miliukov, the Petersburg strikes marked a turning point in the Russian revolutionary movement. 'The Russian "masses", up to that time voiceless and silent, appear now for the first time on the political stage and make their first attempt to speak in their own name.'[11] This newly independent involvement by the masses marked a fundamental difference from the situation faced by earlier revolutionaries, such as Lenin's brother Alexander.

Lenin himself had been arrested months before the culmination of the strike movement in summer 1896 and did not have much to do with it. Like Miliukov he stressed that the socialists should not be held responsible for the St Petersburg strikes. As Lenin put it, 'strikes do not break out because socialist instigators come on the scene, but socialists come on the scene because strikes have started up, the struggle of the workers against the capitalists has started up'.[12] Yet all the more did the strikes reassure him that his wager on 'another way', the Social Democratic way, was paying off. The merger predicted by Kautsky *was* taking place and already having an unprecedented impact, since the mighty tsarist government had been forced to make concessions by passing the law of 2 June 1897 that limited working hours.

Lenin saw the whole episode as confirmation that his heroic scenario was not the idle dream of an impotent revolutionary, for it was turning into reality before his eyes. The factory workers were ready to play the role assigned to them. Once they were aware of their interests, they were ready to fight, and 'no amount of persecution, no wholesale arrests and deportations, no grandiose political trials, no hounding of the workers have been of any avail'. The next step was for the advanced workers to stir up the more backward workers. 'Unless the entire mass of Russian workers is enlisted in the struggle for the workers' cause, the advanced workers of the capital cannot hope to win much.'[13]

The successful participation of the nascent socialist underground in the strike movement gave further proof that the Social Democratic strategy could work in tsarist Russia. Perhaps all that the socialists could do for the present was distribute leaflets that announced the aims of the strikes, but these tiny pieces of paper were the thin end of the wedge of political freedom. As Lenin observed, political freedom meant that, in the rest of Europe, 'the press freely prints news about strikes'. Even though no free press existed in Russia, the socialists and their leaflets ensured that the tsarist government could no longer keep strikes secret, as they had always done in the past. Lenin proudly claimed that 'the government saw that it was becoming quite ridiculous to keep silent, since everybody knew about the strikes – and the government too was dragged along behind the rest. The socialist leaflets called the government to account – and the government appeared and gave its account.'[14]

Lenin went out of his way to emphasize the weakness of the Petersburg underground – 'The Union of Struggle, as we know, was founded only in 1895/6 and its appeals to the workers were confined to badly printed broadsheets' – because this weakness was actually a source of encouragement. If such a feeble organization helped to generate an unprecedented strike movement, what could not be accomplished by a properly organized Social Democratic underground? Just by uniting the organizations of at least the major cities – assuming that these organizations enjoyed as much authority among the workers as did the Petersburg Union of Struggle – Russian Social Democracy could become 'a political factor of the highest order in contemporary Russia'.[15] Faced with such intoxicating perspectives, no wonder Lenin's activist friends danced across the kitchen floor.

The Nuts and Bolts of a Dream

On 8 December 1895 Lenin was arrested, along with the other leaders of the Petersburg Union of Struggle, for the crime of 'Social Democratic propaganda among the workers of Petersburg'.[16] Lenin spent over a year in a Petersburg jail until finally receiving his sentence: three years in Siberian exile. He was assigned to the Siberian village of Shushenskoe, not far from Krasnoyarsk, and duly served out his term. Lenin was lucky – Shushenskoe was tolerable, compared to Turukhansk, the far-north village where

Police photographs of Lenin, December 1895.

L. Martov, a fellow founder of the Union of Struggle, ended up. Martov later wrote passionately about the physical, social and political ghastliness of Turukhansk.[17]

The arrest of so many leaders of the Petersburg Union of Struggle put its very existence in doubt. The younger members who had been left at large worked hard to put out proclamations and to keep in contact with the strikers, since continuing to exist was absolutely necessary for Social Democratic prestige. Lenin cheered these efforts from a distance: 'The public prosecutors and gendarmes are already boasting that they have smashed the Union of Struggle. This boast is a lie. The Union of Struggle is intact, despite all the persecution . . . Revolutionaries have perished – long live the revolution!'[18]

The three years in Shushenskoe were productive ones for Lenin professionally, personally and politically. His main professional achievement was a magnum opus giving a Marxist account of (as the title proclaims) *The Development of Capitalism in Russia* (published in 1899). In this book, filled with statistics on everything from flax-growing to the hemp-and-rope trades, he provided his heroic scenario with as strong a factual foundation as he could manage.

His main personal achievement was marrying Nadezhda Krupskaya on 10 July 1898 and settling down to married life. Krupskaya had been one of the cohort of early *praktiki* that Lenin had joined in St Petersburg. She had arrived in that tight-knit community by a different route from Lenin, by volunteering as a teacher in the Sunday education movement. Like everything independent in Russian life, the popular education movement was regarded with suspicion by the government, which looked askance at 'the tendency to raise the level of popular education by means of organizing lectures, libraries, reading-rooms for, and free distribution of, scientific, moral and literary publications among the factory and rural population'. These are the words of

Nadezhda Krupskaya in 1917, disguised as a worker.

the tsarist minister of the interior in 1895, who described people like Krupskaya when he went on to say that 'the distributors of these books are intelligent young people of both sexes, very often still pursuing their studies, who penetrate into the midst of the people [the *narod*] in the capacity of teachers'. All this was very worrisome to the tsarist minister, since it appeared that the popular education movement 'will develop systematically in a way which will not be in accordance with the views of the government'.[19] The government's suspicion of independent popular education had not changed much since the days of Lenin's father, Ilya Ulyanov.

Many years later, Krupskaya described the life she led after she followed Lenin out to Siberia to marry him:

> Before my eyes I see it as if it were real – that time of primordial wholeness and the joy of existence. Everything was somehow close to nature – sorrel plants, mushrooms, hunting, skating – a tight, close group of comrades. We would go on holiday – exactly thirty years ago this was – in Minusinsk – a close circle of comrades/friends, communal outings, singing, a sort of naive joy and togetherness. My mother lived with us, our domestic economy was primordial, close to roughing it – our life was work in common, one and the same feelings and reactions – we received [writings by] Bernstein [the German 'revisionist'], got all worked up and indignant, and so forth. It seems to me that this kind of life is impossible these days. An awful lot happened over thirty years and many burdens have rested on our shoulders.
> There you are – a little bit of lyric poetry . . .[20]

Lenin's main political achievement during his exile was working out an ambitious plan for realizing his dream of a national underground organization that would be 'a political factor of the highest order'. The most detailed exposition of this plan came a few years later in his famous book *What Is to Be Done?* (1902). We must proceed carefully, because latter-day readers of *What Is to Be Done?* have removed Lenin's book from its context and thereby fundamentally distorted its spirit and impact. According to the standard textbook interpretation, Lenin devised an innovative plan of party organization that consciously rejected the model of Western socialist parties such as the German SPD in favour of an updated version of the conspiratorial underground of earlier populist revolutionaries such as *Narodnaya volya*. Driving his new scheme was a compulsive 'worry about workers', that is, Lenin's conviction that workers were inherently reformist and therefore would not, even could not spontaneously support a revolutionary party. He therefore tried to ensure that the party was composed solely of hardened revolutionary intellectuals – or so we are told.

This picture of a dour, jaded, even cynical Lenin stands in striking contrast to the actual romanticism of his heroic scenario. Lenin's vision of party organization was not his personal innovation but rather a systemization of methods collectively worked out by a whole generation of Social Democratic *praktiki*. Through trial and error these anonymous activists tried to import the SPD strategy – inspiring the masses through party campaigns – into the hostile environment of repressive absolutism. His whole scheme was based not on an anxious worry about workers, but on an enthusiastic confidence that the workers would provide crucial support.

Lenin's heroic scenario had its individual features but its basic theme of leadership, as embodied by an inspired agitator or propagandist spreading the word and raising consciousness, was one that excited many people. In 1906, in his famous novel *Mother*, the left-wing writer Maxim Gorky gave narrative form to this collective dream so effectively that his book later became a Soviet icon and was acclaimed as the precursor of 'socialist realism'. In 1917, on the eve of the Bolshevik revolution, Gorky's novel was summarized for American readers by Moissaye Olgin, an émigré with personal experience in the Russian underground. Olgin's summary reveals not so much what the underground was as what it wanted to be. Recall Lenin's ambitious claims for the impact of socialist 'leaflets' or *listki* during the 1896 strikes, and compare them to Olgin's summary of Gorky (*listki* is here translated as 'papers'):

> Soon the streets of the suburb are strewn with 'papers' written with blue ink (hectographically reproduced proclamations). The 'papers' venomously criticize the system in the factory, they tell about labour strikes in Petersburg and Southern Russia, they call the workingmen to unite in defence of their interests. The 'papers' are read and commented upon. The older folks are morose, the younger are delighted, the majority have no confidence in the strength of the workingmen, yet they know the 'papers' are well meant; the papers speak about the sufferings of the working people; they are telling 'the truth'.
>
> A bond of sympathy is established between the secret organization and the bulk of the toilers. The 'papers' appear regularly; they have become necessary to the population. When they fail to appear for a whole week, people are uneasy. None of the 'rank and file' knows the address or the members of the organization, yet its influence grows.[21]

The organizational goal of the SPD-inspired underground is expressed by the last sentence: 'None of the "rank and file" knows the address or the members of the organization, yet its influence grows.' Is this possible? Can a secret organization really have growing mass influence? The solution to this problem worked out by a generation of Social Democratic activists can be called the *threads strategy*, as set forth in 1906 by M. Liadov, a Bolshevik who broke with Lenin some years later. According to Liadov the challenge facing the underground was 'to expand as much as possible the framework of a secret organization, and, while preserving intact the *konspiratsiia* character of the [party] staff, connect it with a whole series of threads to the mass'.[22]

The word *konspiratsiia* is key for understanding the logic of the threads strategy. It does *not* mean 'conspiracy' (in Russian, *zagovor*). The old populist underground was based on conspiracy – that is, a restrictive secret organization aimed at a political overthrow, a high-level assassination or the like. This kind of underground was therefore only a means for carrying out the goal of a successful conspiracy. Thus conspiracy was required for any revolutionary overthrow of autocracy that *lacked* mass organization. In contrast, *konspiratsiia* was required for any revolutionary overthrow of autocracy that *included* mass organization. Although *konspiratsiia* was derived from the French word *conspiration*, it had acquired in Russia the strongly contrasted meaning of all the practical rules of conduct needed to elude the police, even while preserving the threads connecting the organization to a wider community. *Konspiratsiia* can be defined as 'the fine art of not getting arrested'. In contrast to a conspiracy, *konspiratsiia* was only a means toward an end, namely, keeping the underground organization and its threads in existence.

In a dispute with veteran populist Petr Lavrov that Lenin conducted during his Siberian exile, Lenin energetically rejected the strategy of conspiracy and associated methods such as individual terror. Old-timers like Lavrov automatically equated anti-tsarist political struggle with bomb-throwing conspiracies. They therefore assumed that the Social Democrats, who rejected conspiracy, were not serious about achieving political freedom by revolutionary means. But there was a real alternative to old-fashioned conspiracy (responded Lenin): an underground organization connected by a variety of threads to a mass constituency, one that manages to stay in existence through strict observance of the rules of *konspiratsiia*.[23]

The viability of the *konspiratsiia* underground was crucial for the success of Lenin's 'other way'. The class leadership evoked by his heroic scenario required an underground organization that both eluded police *and* maintained contact with the workers. No wonder Lenin spent so much thought on the details of how this could be accomplished – they were the nuts and bolts of a dream.

Anyone who argued for the workability of the threads strategy needed to make some very optimistic assumptions. Typically, Lenin made these assumptions with gusto and scorned the sceptics and 'philistines' who had less exalted expectations. One such assumption was the existence of a supportive worker milieu that would pick up the threads thrown out by the *konspiratsiia* underground. When the revolutionaries of the 1870s went to the people, the puzzled peasants promptly turned these strange beings over to the police. When the *praktiki* of the 1890s went to the workers, they gradually found enough sympathy to allow them to operate. The Social Democrats were no longer alien beings with incomprehensible schemes, but familiar social types with a relevant (even if not always accepted) message. Without the supportive worker milieu, all the methods that the *praktiki* had painfully elaborated for foiling the police would have meant nothing.

In his advocacy of a particularly ambitious thread connecting underground and workers – a national party newspaper – Lenin insisted on the existence of this worker milieu. True (he admitted) producing and distributing a newspaper of national scope is a difficult task – much more difficult than the tasks taken up by the older Russian underground, which did not even dream about mass distribution of a newspaper. But, continued Lenin, the target audience today makes the task much more manageable: industrial districts where workers make up almost the entire population, so that 'the worker is factually master of the situation with hundreds of ways to outwit the vigilance of the police'.[24] (Note that the sceptical 'worry about workers' so often ascribed to Lenin would have radically undercut all his arguments about the viability of a *konspiratsiia* underground.)

The plausibility of the underground threads strategy also required the validity of another optimistic assumption: a steady supply of people both *heroic* enough to risk career, health, freedom and even life for the cause, and *self-disciplined* enough to learn the necessary skills of *konspiratsiia* and to act in strict accordance with them – not always the most likely combination of qualities. Someone who combined both these qualities was the ideal 'professional revolutionary' – a functional necessity of an underground specifically of the *konspiratsiia* type. The conspiratorial revolutionary of the earlier populist underground was meant to *replace* a mass spd-like party, deemed impossible under Russian conditions. In contrast, the professional revolutionary of the *konspiratsiia* underground was supposed to make something resembling a mass spd-like party possible, even under Russian conditions.

The term 'professional revolutionary' in this meaning was coined by Lenin himself in *What Is to Be Done?* (1902) and then quickly adopted by the entire socialist underground. Yet Lenin's own relation to this term is rather curious. The image of the professional revolutionary has two aspects: the poetry of daring and self-sacrifice vs. the prose of competence and self-discipline. At least in *What Is to Be Done?*, Lenin was much more interested in the prosaic side. The romantic image goes back to Rakhmetov, the ascetic revolutionary saint pictured in Nikolai Chernyshevsky's novel of 1863, *What Is to Be Done?*. Lenin was a great admirer of Chernyshevsky, and his use of this title for his book on party organization was not a coincidence. But the underground certainly did not need Lenin to see themselves as Rakhmetovs. One of Lenin's most vociferous opponents, Aleksandr Martynov, later recalled his own hero-worship of Rakhmetov, whom he imitated when a schoolboy by slowly crushing cigarettes on his own hand.[25]

While in exile in Siberia – no doubt brooding on the damage done to the Petersburg Union of Struggle by the police – Lenin began to insist that underground *praktiki* needed to learn their own trade properly and thoroughly. He listed in very specific detail the functions needed to operate a *konspiratsiia* underground: agitation, distribution of leaflets and other illegal literature, organizers of worker study circles, correspondents reporting on worker grievances, security against government spies, setting up *konspirativnyi* apartments for secret meetings, transmitting instructions, collecting for funds and so on. He then argued that 'the smaller and more specific the job undertaken by the individual person or individual group, the greater will be the chance that they will think things out, do the job properly and guarantee it best against failure [and at the same time] the harder it will be for the police and gendarmes to keep track of the revolutionaries.' True, this kind of work may seem 'inconspicuous, monotonous . . . a grim and rigid routine'.[26] To be so prosaic required a special kind of heroism.

The chapter of Lenin's *What Is to Be Done?* in which he introduced the term *revoliutsioner po professii* was devoted to pushing this same theme. A translation of this term that brings out Lenin's underlying metaphor is 'revolutionary by trade', since the word *professiia* at the time meant primarily the trade of a skilled worker (a 'trade union' was a *professionalnyi soiuz*). Lenin's coinage was thus meant to evoke the image of a specialized and skilled worker in an efficient organization. The image that emerges from Lenin's unsystematic use of the metaphor is the designedly prosaic one of a *praktik* honing his skills in his chosen trade.

Lenin's coinage rapidly became an indispensable part of the vocabulary of the entire underground, partly because the 'revolutionary by trade' was a functional necessity of *any* underground of the *konspiratsiia* type. But the prosaic 'revolutionary by trade' was also the romantic and daring 'professional revolutionary'. A few years after the publication of *What Is to Be Done?* a leader of the Socialist Revolutionary party, Victor Chernov, described the professional revolutionary as 'a roving apostle of socialism, a knight who punishes evil-doers . . . his life-style is *konspiratsiia*, his sport is a contest with the police in cleverness and elusiveness'. He glories in his escapes from prison.[27] Thus for the underground as a whole, the professional revolutionary gains authority because he is tough enough to be arrested and to escape. For Lenin in *What Is to Be Done?* the revolutionary by trade gains authority because he is smart enough not to get arrested in the first place.

Yet Lenin would not be Lenin if his insistence on the professional qualifications of the underground *praktiki* were not closely tied to his heroic scenario of inspiring leadership. In *What Is to Be Done?* professional training is a vital but not the only trait of the ideal underground activist. Following the SPD example, Lenin's ideal *praktik* will rise from worker ranks. (The idea that Lenin restricted the status of 'revolutionary by trade' to intellectuals has no factual basis and is incompatible with his entire outlook.) Such a *praktik* will acquire broad horizons by working in all parts of the country. He will acquire in this way 'a knowledge of the worker milieu plus a freshness of socialist conviction, combined with a full apprenticeship in his trade', that is, the trade of underground activity. Given such trained agitators, propagandists and organizers from worker ranks, 'no political police in the world will be able to cope with these detachments' of the revolutionary army, since these activists will combine boundless devotion to the revolution with the ability to inspire 'the boundless confidence of the broadest worker mass'.[28] Such were Lenin's boundless promises to the aspiring *praktiki*.

The fact that Lenin became (as one hostile Menshevik leader put it in 1904) 'the idol of the *praktiki*' is therefore not hard to explain.[29] On the one hand Lenin's interest in the nuts-and-bolts problems of the *konspiratsiia* underground showed an appreciation of their difficulties that was rare among the intellectual leaders of the party. On the other his heroic scenario provided the activists with a romantic self-image of leaders who were capable of inspiring boundless confidence. In 1904 both supporters and opponents concurred in their view of Lenin as the chosen voice of the *praktiki*. In 1905 Alexander Potresov – a former colleague of Lenin, but by this time a determined foe – argued that he owed his popularity to the uncanny accuracy with which he embodied the grandiose and pathetically unrealistic self-image of the underground activists.[30] Much later, in 1920, Stalin praised Lenin's early organizational writings because they 'completely corresponded to Russian realities and generalized in masterly fashion the organizational experience of the best *praktiki*' (among whom he numbered himself).[31]

When Lenin came up with his basic ideas of party organization, he was in Siberian exile. When he wrote *What Is to Be Done?* five years later, he was an émigré in Western Europe. Yet the emotional link between him and the *praktiki* toiling away in Russian towns is revealed by a letter Lenin received from a party comrade soon after the publication of *What Is to Be Done?* in 1902. After talking with some Social Democratic 'purposive workers', I. I. Radchenko wrote to Lenin:

> Before me sat the Lenin type – people longing for the revolutionary trade [*professiia*]. I was happy for Lenin, who sits a million miles away, barricaded by bayonets, cannon, borders, border guards and other features of the autocracy – and he sees how people work here on the shop floor, what they need and what they will become. Believe it, my friends, soon we will see our Bebels [August Bebel rose from worker origins to become the leader of German Social Democracy]. Genuine lathe turners /revolutionaries . . . doing everything for the cause with the profound faith that 'I *will* do this'. I say it one more time: this was the happiest moment of my life.[32]

Iskra and the Heroic Scenario

While Lenin served his time in far Siberia the Social Democratic underground was making progress. Against all odds a Social Democratic movement had established itself by the late 1890s in a myriad of individual towns all across Russia. In March 1898 a genuine step toward national unification was taken by a congress in Minsk at which the Russian Social Democratic Worker Party (RSDWP) was founded. In most respects this First Congress was premature: all of its members were promptly arrested and no central party institutions were put in place. But the party now had at least a virtual existence – the local 'unions of struggle' began to think of themselves as committees of a national, if still notional, organization. Perhaps the time was right for realizing Lenin's dream of a Russian Social Democracy that would be 'a political factor of the highest order'.

Lenin could only observe developments from the sidelines, but he was eager to reach the end of his Siberian exile and get down to work. He had his own ideas about how to turn Russian Social Democracy into a national presence and he was champing at the bit to put them into practice. As soon as his term elapsed in 1899 Lenin met with Martov (also just released from Siberia) and Potresov (who was more of a littérateur and less of a *praktik* than the other two). Having concerted their plans they spirited themselves abroad in July 1900 (the fake passport obtained for this occasion may have been the origin of 'Lenin' as a pseudonym). Before settling down in Munich, Lenin, Martov and Potresov held meetings in Geneva with the older émigrés of the Liberation of Labour group: Georgy Plekhanov, Vera Zasulich and Pavel Axelrod. After a rocky start, due to Plekhanov's personal prickliness, the first goal of Lenin's scheme came to fruition: the all-Russian political newspaper *Iskra* was launched in December 1900.

Iskra would not win any journalistic awards today for layout and design. An issue usually consisted of six pages of three columns

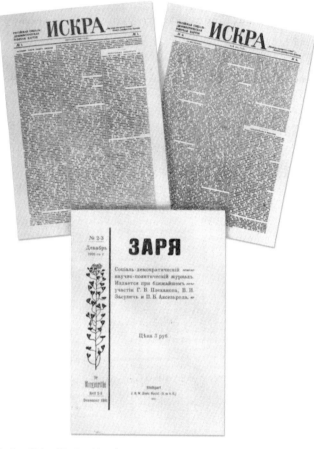

Copies of *Iskra* (The Spark) and its sister journal *Zaria* (The Dawn).

each, each column filled to the brim with small type and big words. Some observers complained that it was over the head of worker readers, but the editors were confident that at least the 'advanced' and 'purposive' workers were up to it and that they could channel the message to other readers. Because it was written, edited and printed abroad, it could come out with a regularity that broke all underground records. Between the first issue in December 1900 and the publication of *What Is to Be Done?* in early 1902, fifteen issues had come out. During the three years Lenin was on the editorial board (he left late in 1903) there were 51 issues.

Lenin's ambitious hope was that *Iskra* would not just be another example of émigré protest literature but would be connected with many threads to actual developments in Russia. The local underground committees would provide *Iskra*'s editors with journalistic copy on breaking news, while the *Iskra* organization would do its damnedest to get copies of *Iskra* to the committees for further distribution. So began the cat-and-mouse game of false passports, double-bottomed suitcases, secret printing presses and roving emissaries that often ended in confusion and despair, but also resulted in giving all-Russia significance to *Iskra*. Osip Piatnitsky, one of the young 'revolutionaries by trade' entrusted with the task of setting up this underground distribution network, later recalled how he used the services of Lithuanian religious groups who were already smuggling books across the border (books in Lithuanian were prohibited in Russia). This de facto alliance is revealing. Both the Lithuanians and the Social Democrats were determined to spread the good news, as they respectively saw it.[33]

Iskra became the centre of Lenin's life. In 1902, soon after the completion of *What Is to Be Done?*, the German printers decided that printing *Iskra* was too risky. So Lenin and Krupskaya moved to London, where they lived from April 1902 to April 1903.

Lenin, along with Krupskaya, was at the centre of the *Iskra* enterprise: getting people to write articles, writing many of them himself, conducting correspondence, overseeing transport and even putting individual issues to bed at the printer. No task was too menial for Lenin if it meant making the great plan a reality. In many ways the *Iskra* enterprise was Lenin's most successful leadership undertaking. Lenin's devotion to *Iskra* was closely bound up with his heroic scenario of inspiring class leadership. Newspapers

Lenin's cramped office in London, 1902–3, loaned to him by the Twentieth Century Press in order to edit issues of *Iskra*. The office is unchanged at 37 Clerkenwell Green, a building that today also houses the Marx Memorial Library.

had always been a central feature of the SPD model. Furthermore, *Iskra* played a crucial role in Lenin's scheme for creating working party institutions on a national scale. Finally, Lenin's heroic scenario lay behind the image of contemporary Russia that was ceaselessly propagated by *Iskra* and other publications of the *Iskra* team.

Nothing symbolized the German SPD more than the multitude of newspapers that helped propagate its message. By the outbreak of war in 1914 the German party owned more than eighty newspapers. But publishing an illegal newspaper in Russia presented a formidable, almost insuperable obstacle for local organizations. *Rabochaia mysl* (Worker Thought) in Petersburg and *Rabochaia gazeta* (Worker News) in Saratov were admirable efforts, but they were of poor technical quality, appeared irregularly and were subject to police repression. Lenin was therefore not the only one calling for a nationwide party newspaper that would point to 'the *common* reasons for the oppression of the workers, to the political system and the necessity of struggle against it'.[34]

Iskra also had a specific role to play in Lenin's scheme to create a national party structure. The challenge that faced the new *konspiratsiia* underground was different in essence from the one that had faced the old-style conspiratorial underground. In the old underground a central group strove to create local offshoots, whereas in the Social Democratic underground isolated local groups were trying to find their way to achieve central coordination. In exile Lenin had worked out an ingenious scheme for using a national underground newspaper such as *Iskra* to meet this challenge. *Iskra* could not be the official party newspaper, not yet anyway, because there existed no official party institutions of any kind. To erect a national party authority you needed relatively homogeneous local committees – but to obtain homogeneous committees, you needed a common party authority. How to escape from this vicious circle? Here's how: begin with the creation of an all-Russian political newspaper, published abroad, since the difficulty and risks of publishing it in Russia were too great. At first this newspaper would admittedly be the product of a self-appointed and unauthorized group but it would have the undeniable virtue of actually existing, of actually coming out regularly, many times a year, with at least adequate technical quality.

This newspaper would then make an appeal to the local committees in Russia to become integral partners in its creation (through providing factual material and reports) and distribution. Thus, for the first time, the committees would be working together on a national project. The organization needed to transport the newspapers would be the embryo of a national organization of professional revolutionaries that linked centre and localities. Furthermore, this newspaper would create programmatic unity by preaching a consistent line to which the various committees could adhere. The politically oriented agitation of the newspaper would also strengthen nationwide unity, since political issues tended more than economic grievances to be common, national ones. If all went well, the virtual authority claimed by the newspaper would create enough practical and programmatic unity among the scattered local committees that their representatives could come together and act effectively to create an actual authority. The newspaper, hitherto a private affair, could then become the sanctioned, legitimate voice of a genuinely functioning set of central institutions.

Such was Lenin's ambitious plan. In the meantime *Iskra* was already helping to make Social Democracy a political factor on the national scale simply by propagating a unified, all-Russian message. *Iskra* portrayed the situation in Russia as seen through the prism of Lenin's heroic scenario. The autocracy was on the verge of collapse. All sections of society were thoroughly disgusted with the clumsy monster. The workers, the peasants, the entrepreneurs, the nationalities, even many landowners – all had turned against the tsar. Discontent was turning into protest and protest into action, and the main impulse for the growing intensity of the revolutionary crisis was the mass actions of the workers. Their heroic protest, not just against capitalists but directly against tsarist despotism, was galvanizing the rest of society into a realization that the autocracy *could* be overthrown. And once this realization took hold, the autocracy's days were numbered.

The same heroic picture of Russia in crisis permeates the pages of *What Is to Be Done?* (1902), later described by Lenin as a compendium of the *Iskra* outlook. The book is filled with nuts-and-bolts organizational strategies but what gives life to these prosaic arguments is the poetry of the exalted mission imposed by history on the Russian *konspiratsiia* underground. *What Is to Be Done?* portrays the Russian workers as so eager to fight that they continually outstrip the capacity of the Social Democrats to provide the requisite knowledge and organization. The workers continually push forth leaders from their own ranks – leaders who are able to inspire their fellows to undertake the noble task of freeing Russia from shameful despotism. As a result the workers as a class are on the move and they are galvanizing all of Russian society.

Lenin's own inspiration in *What Is to Be Done?* is the mighty German Social Democratic party, whose example is invoked much more often and more concretely than is the example of the earlier Russian conspiratorial underground. Lenin assured his readers that the empirically worked-out application of the SPD model to Russian conditions – the threads strategy – was perfectly workable, if the *praktiki* would only hone their own professional skills. All that was necessary was to combine tight *konspiratsiia* at one level with a looser and more open type of organization at levels closer to the workers. Both ends of the threads thrown out by the underground would be protected. Secrecy would insulate the local party institutions from the police, while the supportive worker milieu would insulate activists directly in contact with workers.

One of the most famous quotes from *What Is to Be Done?* is the cry: 'give us an organization of revolutionaries – and we will turn Russia around!' This is often taken as a clarion call for a conspiratorial underground: 'Forget about the unreliable workers and concentrate on conspirators recruited from the intelligentsia.' But when Lenin's statement is read in its immediate context it reveals itself as one more manifestation of Lenin's unrepentant confidence in his heroic scenario. Lenin's actual argument is: even back in 1895 the workers were so militant that the weak link in the chain was we ourselves, the Social Democrats. We failed in our job of providing the organization needed to make worker protest effective. How much more true today, when everybody can see the workers are on the move against tsarist absolutism! No wonder Lenin informed the sceptics: 'You brag about your practicality and you don't see (a fact known to any Russian *praktik*) what miracles for the revolutionary cause can be brought about not only by a [local Social Democratic] circle but by a lone individual.'[35]

What Is to Be Done? focuses on the underground's role in the epic national struggle against the tsar that Lenin saw in his mind's eye. But *What Is to Be Done?* is only one part of Lenin's output during his years with *Iskra* (1900–1903). He also wrote scores of articles for *Iskra* and other publications, plus a seventy-page pamphlet entitled *To the Village Poor (An explanation for the peasants of what the Social Democrats want)*. Because this overlooked pamphlet is one of the few pieces Lenin wrote exclusively for a non-party audience, it can be recommended as a very accessible presentation of Lenin's heroic scenario. If *To the Village Poor* were as well-known as *What Is to Be Done?* the heart of Lenin's vision would be much better understood than it is.

The writings of the *Iskra* period covered a wide range of topics, but all of them were informed by the fiery energy of Lenin's commitment to his 'other way'. Among the subjects treated are:

The overall crisis facing tsarism and its ineffective attempts to stave off its swiftly approaching doom.

Heroic worker protest and its effect on the rest of Russian society.

The peasantry as an integral part of the anti-tsarist coalition.

The nationalism of ethnic minorities, to be encouraged as a force subverting tsarism but discouraged as a centrifugal force within the party.

Individual terrorism as an outmoded and harmful revolutionary expedient.

The deficiencies of the liberals and the Socialist Revolutionaries (SRs), the emerging rivals to Social Democracy for leadership of the anti-tsarist revolution.

As we saw earlier, *Iskra* was also meant to be a springboard toward achieving ideological and organizational unity among the scattered committees. This part of Lenin's plan was also put into practice, but the reality was a lot messier than his original picture.

True, more and more committees officially endorsed *Iskra* as their spokesman. But this bandwagon effect was achieved at the cost of hurtful internal struggles, sharp practices on all sides and local reorganizations that, although intended to help put workers onto local committees, were carried out in such a way that many workers felt seriously aggrieved.

In April 1903, Lenin and Krupskaya moved rather reluctantly from London to Geneva, in deference to the wish of the other *Iskra* editors to be together in one city. By this time enough momentum had been created to organize an acceptably representative Second Congress, and RSDWP members met abroad in August 1903. The Congress opened in Brussels but was then forced by pressure from the Belgian police to move to London. As Social Democrats often said to console themselves during the bitterness of the ensuing factional struggle, the Second Congress did have some lasting positive achievements. Not only were central party institutions finally created, but a consensus on basic programmatic and tactical perspectives was laid down. Social Democracy had become and remained a coherent all-Russian presence.

But Lenin's plan hit a completely unexpected snag at the very moment of its fulfilment. The *Iskra* editorial board fell apart in ugly mutual recriminations. The divisive issues were dense and tangled, combining personal animosities, organizational jockeying for position and genuine difference in revolutionary tactics. These deeper differences only gradually rose to the surface, and resulted in the split between Bolsheviks and Mensheviks that dominated Social Democratic politics for the next decade. At the Second Congress in August 1903 Lenin had been the dominant party leader. But by the end of the year he was completely isolated – forced to leave the *Iskra* editorial board and on very bad terms with all his former colleagues (see chapter Three). For a while it looked like Lenin's first decade as a party leader might be his last.

According to the banner sentence of 1894 the opening act of Lenin's world-historical drama would see the Russian 'purposive worker' imbued with the 'idea of the historical role of the Russian worker', namely, to act as leader of the *narod*. Furthermore, 'durable organisations [would be] created among the workers that transform the present uncoordinated economic war of the workers into a purposive class struggle'. Something like this actually happened. The Russian version of Kautsky's canonical merger of socialism and the worker movement was the *konspiratsiia* underground, that unique and underappreciated historical creation of a whole generation of *praktiki*. Lenin's individual role in this creation was, first, his summation of the logic of the threads strategy; second, his eloquent defence of the optimistic assumptions needed to sustain faith in the viability of a truly Social Democratic underground; and third, his ingenious plan for creating national party structures. As always a cold-eyed look at reality will reveal the yawning gap between the actual *konspiratsiia* underground and its heroic self-inscription into the narrative of Lenin's banner sentence. Certainly for Lenin himself his first decade ended in bitterness and seeming isolation. Yet his dream, far-fetched as it may have been, was a historical reality because people believed in it.

In a climactic passage from *What Is to Be Done?* Lenin evoked his heroic 'other way' as he outlined his ambitious project of using the newfangled methods of European Social Democracy in order to realize the dreams of Russian revolutionaries such as his brother Alexander. Lenin uses Alexander Zheliabov, a leader of the *Narodnaya volya* group that assassinated the tsar in 1881, to symbolize the Russian revolutionary tradition; he uses August Bebel, a worker who became the top leader of the German SPD, to symbolize Social Democracy:

> If we genuinely succeed in getting all or a significant majority of local committees, local groups and circles actively to take up the

common work, we would in short order be able to have a weekly newspaper, regularly distributed in tens of thousands of copies throughout Russia. This newspaper would be a small part of a huge bellows that blows up each flame of class struggle and popular indignation into a common fire. Around this task – in and of itself a very small and even innocent one but one that is a regular and, in the full meaning of the word, a *common* task – an army of experienced fighters would systematically be recruited and trained. Among the ladders and scaffolding of this common organizational construction would soon rise up Social Democratic Zheliabovs from among our revolutionaries, Russian Bebels from our workers, who would be pushed forward and then take their place at the head of a mobilized army and would raise up the whole *narod* to settle accounts with the shame and curse of Russia.

That is what we must dream about![36]

3

A People's Revolution

'During the whirlwind [of the 1905 revolution], the
proletarian, the railwayman, the peasant, the mutinous
soldier, have driven all Russia forward with the speed of
a locomotive.' Lenin, 1906

Bolshevism, as a distinct current in Russian Social Democracy,
arose in the years 1904–14. During those years Bolshevism was
a Russian answer to Russian problems. Later, when Bolshevism
acquired a wider meaning, Lenin coined the term 'Old Bolshevism'
as a label for the earlier period. 'Old Bolshevism' is a useful term
that we will employ in later chapters. But for now Old Bolshevism
is the only Bolshevism there is, so we shall dispense with the
qualifying adjective.

In Lenin's banner sentence of 1894 the crucial central episode
of the heroic scenario is described in the following words: 'the
Russian WORKER, elevated to the head of all democratic elements,
will overthrow absolutism'. These few words contain the essence of
Bolshevism during its first decade, and we shall spend this chapter
unpacking their meaning. We must first ask: what is the role of
this episode in the overall heroic scenario? The answer: to open up
the road to socialist revolution by removing the obstacle of tsarist
absolutism. The more thoroughly the revolution did its job, the
swifter would be the journey to the final goal. Therefore, the party's
goal should be revolution 'to the end' (*do kontsa*), that is, 'to the

'Russian People in the Grip of Autocracy', from M. J. Olgin's *The Soul of the Russian Revolution* (1917).

absolute destruction of monarchical despotism' and its replacement by a democratic republic.[1]

According to the logic of Lenin's heroic scenario, the only way to successfully carry out the democratic revolution 'to the end' is for the urban proletariat to be the head, the leader, the *vozhd* of all the 'democratic elements', that is, all the social groups with a stake in attaining full political freedom. The Russian revolution could only succeed as a *narodnaia revoliutsiia*, a people's revolution. In order for the proletariat to play its destined leadership role it had to spread its message far and wide. And the only way to do that was through the institutions of the *konspiratsiia* underground. The Russian revolution could only succeed if these channels were kept open.

During the years 1905–7 Russia underwent a profound revolution and the tsar was forced to grant a significant measure of political freedom. When Lenin viewed these events through the lens of his heroic scenario he arrived at the following conclusions: The 1905 revolution was a vast, mighty people's revolution. Unfortunately, the revolution was not able to go all the way 'to the end' by replacing tsarism with a democratic republic. It nevertheless achieved great things and represented a tremendous vindication of Social Democratic expectations. The decade-long consciousness-raising activity of the underground party paid off because the proletariat did indeed act as leader of the *narod*.

Lenin's advice for the future was based on this reading of the events of 1905. The Russian Social Democrats needed to prepare for a decisive repetition of the 1905 revolution – one which would carry out the revolution to the end by creating a provisional government based on the workers and peasants. Only a government based on these classes ('revolutionary democratic dictatorship of the workers and peasants') would be able to install a democratic republic and beat back the counterrevolution with the necessary ruthlessness. The best way to prepare for this second people's revolution was to remain loyal to the strategy that made the first one possible: the leadership role of the urban workers ('hegemony of the proletariat') and an energetic commitment to spread the socialist good news despite government repression.

The official slogans of Bolshevism used learned foreign-sounding phrases such as 'hegemony of the proletariat' and 'revolutionary democratic dictatorship of the workers and peasants'. But the inner meaning of these phrases is profoundly Russian and arises from an interpretation of the revolutions of 1905–7 in terms of Lenin's heroic scenario. Even Bolsheviks who otherwise were opponents of Lenin subscribed to this core platform.

Lenin's political life during the whole decade was therefore a fight for the meaning of the revolution of 1905–7. A review of the events of these tumultuous years is essential background for Lenin's personal biography.

The Revolution of 1905–7

The immediate background to the revolution was the shock administered to Russian society by international competition at its most unforgiving. War with Japan began with a Japanese attack on Russian forces on 8 February 1904. Historians have recently suggested that this overlooked conflict should really be called World War Zero, the first of the global conflicts that defined the twentieth century.[2] As Russia's military lurched from disaster to disaster, Russian society – never terribly enthusiastic about the war to begin with – moved toward revolutionary disaffection.

Against the background of growing military defeat the powerful tsarist government began to look shaky and unsure. On 28 July 1904 the widely hated Minister of the Interior Vyacheslav von Plehve was assassinated by Socialist Revolutionary terrorists. The government responded, not in its usual manner of clamping down, but by offering concessions to public opinion. Liberal forces in elite society took advantage of the new atmosphere by unleashing a 'banquet campaign' in autumn 1904 which featured respectable pillars of society offering toasts that turned into subversive speeches.

The event that really sparked off the revolution of 1905, from the Social Democratic point of view, was Bloody Sunday (9 January 1905), when the tsarist government, in its ineffable wisdom, chose to open fire on a peaceful crowd that wanted to present a petition to the tsar asking for basic freedoms. The resulting massacre did more to confirm the Social Democratic message than years of propaganda. In the months that followed events in Russia moved closer to a revolutionary explosion.

The rhythm of the revolution waxed and waned over the spring and summer of 1905 but the climax came with the massive events of October 1905, when a strike started by railwaymen became a general one. Russian society was shut down and the government, panicky and isolated, responded by issuing the Manifesto of 17 October, in which the tsar graciously conceded basic political freedoms to his subjects. The final months of 1905 became known as the 'days of freedom', since political activity was for a short while unrestricted by police or censor.

After the October Manifesto the question confronting the revolutionary forces was: do we now turn our attention to protecting and using what we have achieved, or do we press on 'to the end'? The answer of the more impatient revolutionary elements came in the form of the Moscow uprising of December 1905, when the Moscow workers mounted an 'armed insurrection' that managed to hold out for a week of heavy fighting. The Moscow uprising was the last of the classic nineteenth-century barricade struggles between elite and people, but one that was fought with a new twentieth-century intensity. Barricades were put up, but the insurgents mainly resorted to guerrilla warfare – hit and run attacks that relied on the sympathy of the city population (not just the workers) for support and cover. In response the government trained artillery fire on the city as a whole. The leadership for the uprising came from the Moscow Bolshevik committee, although the Mensheviks and the Socialist Revolutionaries had participated enthusiastically.

The ultimate defeat of the Moscow uprising was one of the many signs that the tide of revolution had begun to ebb. The St Petersburg Soviet – a class-based elective 'council' that was a prototype for 'soviet power' in 1917 – was disbanded, and its leadership (including Lev Trotsky) arrested. Although peasant rebellions were still going strong in 1906, the punitive expeditions of the government were already beginning to quell peasant disorders. The

A satirical look at restrictions on the Duma, 1906–7, from Olgin's *The Soul of the Russian Revolution*.

government acted on its promise to create an elective legislature or Duma, but it refused to work with the liberal and peasant parties that made up the Duma majority. It therefore closed down the first Duma (elected in March 1906) and then the second Duma (elected in early 1907). Only in June 1907 was a new, highly restrictive electoral law imposed, allowing the government to get a Duma with which it could work.

The new electoral law in 1907 was imposed by an unconstitutional coup carried out by the newly appointed minister Petr Stolypin. Stolypin was the outstanding figure of the new post-revolutionary regime, representing both its repressive face (the nooses that were used to hang peasant rebels were called 'Stolypin neckties') and its reformist face (the 'Stolypin land reform' was aimed at transforming property relations in peasant agriculture).

By the end of 1907 the revolution was over and the 'Stolypin era' in full swing, but the passions of the revolutionary era still informed Russian political debate. What were the successes of the revolution? What were its failures? Could a second edition be expected any time soon? If so, how to prepare for it? If not, how to adjust to the new post-revolutionary context? Bolshevism was defined by its answers to questions like these.

Lenin and the Revolution

At the beginning of 1904, when we last saw Lenin, he was living in Geneva and more politically isolated than he would ever be again. After resigning from the *Iskra* editorial board in late 1903, he had no journalistic outlet in which to make his case – a situation that was never to recur – and was barely hanging on to any official position in the Russian Social Democratic party. Perhaps his career as a leader was over. Grigory Zinoviev later recalled how the older leader Georgy Plekhanov frightened young Social Democratic émigrés such as himself who were leaning toward Lenin:

> You follow him, but in a couple of weeks the line he is now carrying out will make him good for nothing but to scare crows in gardens. Lenin picked up the banner of struggle against me, Plekhanov, against Zasulich, Deutsch. Do you really not under-stand that this is an unequal struggle? Lenin is finished. From the moment he broke with us, the elders, the founders of the Liberation of Labour group, his song was sung.[3]

But Lenin was not as isolated as he seemed to the émigré community in Switzerland. Many of those actually running the party in

Russia saw Lenin as their spokesperson and could not understand why he was no longer in the party leadership. Bolshevism as an organized faction within the Russian Social Democratic party arose in the first place through Lenin's efforts to mobilize this support. Nevertheless, we should not give too much weight to the various accusations and counteraccusations that accompanied the growing split between the Bolsheviks and the Mensheviks in 1903–4. Pavel Axelrod, leader of the Mensheviks in 1904, did not accuse Lenin of any ideological heresy. Rather (as he wrote to Kautsky trying to explain the Lenin phenomenon), Lenin was just a troublemaker who unfortunately was the 'idol' of the underground *praktiki* in Russia. For his part, Lenin later stressed that Bolshevism acquired its real content during the 1905 revolution.[4]

Despite the war, Lenin's attention during 1904 was turned toward disputes within the party, and he wrote practically nothing all year besides factional polemics. But even prior to the outbreak of the revolution in January 1905, Lenin could not imagine a revolution in any terms other than that of the proletariat leading the *narod*. Writing in late 1904 Lenin explained in his own way the relative quiescence in the militant activity of the Russian worker movement in the year prior to the revolution. 'The proletariat is holding itself back, as it were, carefully observing the surrounding environment, gathering its forces, and deciding the question whether or not the moment for the decisive struggle for freedom has come.' But this state of affairs could not last. Lenin was confident that military disaster in the war against Japan would lead to a tremendous outburst of protest from the *narod*. When this happened, 'the proletariat will rise and take its stand at the head of the uprising to fight and achieve freedom for the entire *narod* and to secure for the working class the possibility of waging the open and broad struggle for socialism, a struggle enriched by the whole experience of Europe'.[5]

Even after the revolution broke out Lenin focused primarily on organizing a new party congress that would consolidate Bolshevik control of the party. Lenin got his congress, which met in London during April 1905, but since it was boycotted by the Mensheviks, it became a purely Bolshevik affair – indeed, it is regarded by some as the founding congress of Bolshevism. The delegates sent abroad by local party committees in Russia ambitiously encouraged each other to focus on armed insurrection, and then dispersed back home.

After London, Lenin remained in Geneva and returned to Russia only after the amnesty that accompanied the October Manifesto. He arrived in Petersburg on 8 November, although, since habits of *konspiratsiia* died hard, he cautiously disguised himself to 'look more like a minor Petersburg official than like himself'.[6] In the last months of 1905 Lenin participated in the work of the Petersburg Soviet, but continued to give his main attention to party reorganization.

The militancy of 1905 had led to considerable grass-roots unity between the two Social Democratic factions, often in a Bolshevik direction, and Lenin felt that the party could now be unified in a satisfactory way. At one party congress in Stockholm in 1906 – called the 'Unity Congress' in a triumph of hope over experience – the Mensheviks were in a majority. At the next congress, in London in 1907, the Bolsheviks were in a majority. But these seesaws hardly mattered. The Bolsheviks and the Mensheviks were by now separated not only by personal animosities but by deep differences that often revealed themselves in disputes over the proper way to remember 1905. According to a joke current at the time, some police officers escorting a Menshevik and a Bolshevik to prison wanted to go off for a drink. They decided they could safely leave their two prisoners without supervision. Anybody else would have used the opportunity to make an escape, but a Menshevik and a Bolshevik would invariably spend the whole time arguing with each other.

In 1906–7 Lenin lived in some ways not unlike that of a Western socialist party leader. He spoke to public gatherings in St Petersburg,

Vasa Cottage at Kuokkala, now Repino, north of St Petersburg in the semi-autonomous Grand Duchy of Finland, where Lenin hid from the police in 1906–7.

wrote articles for the legal press, and consulted with fellow activists. But 'the days of freedom' of late 1905 were becoming a fading memory as the tsarist government systematically rolled back the space for legal opposition. By August 1906 Lenin found it convenient to move from Petersburg to nearby Finland, where the political situation was somewhat more liberal. It was a sign of the times when at the end of 1907 Lenin's tome on agrarian policy was 'arrested', that is, all copies were confiscated (it was not legally published until 1917). In order not to meet a similar fate himself, Lenin (and later his wife, whom he met en route), left for Geneva and embarked on his second emigration period.

In early 1906 Lenin directly revealed his own deep emotional reaction to the revolution he was living through and, as usual, the occasion was a polemic against his life-long enemy, philistine scepticism. Lenin's target was a liberal professor who bemoaned what he called 'the revolutionary whirlwind', a destructive and unhinged period during which the unreason of the mob left no room for insight and intellect, as opposed to the safe and sane days of reasonable and constructive progress. Lenin exploded against this attempt to 'spatter revolutionary periods and revolutionary methods of creating history with the slime of philistine indignation, condemnation and regret'.[7] In response Lenin made a stirring defence of the 'insight of the masses' during 1905.

Led by the urban workers, the masses had effectively wielded a 'purely proletarian weapon, the mass political strike, on a scale unprecedented even in the most developed countries'. They had set up new authoritative institutions: the myriad soviets, peasant committees and other organizations that had spontaneously sprung up during the revolution. These new institutions were distinguished by extreme democratism: 'a public authority [*vlast*] open to all, one that carried out all its functions before the eyes of the masses, that was accessible to the masses, springing directly from the masses, and a direct and immediate instrument of the mass of the *narod*, of its will'.[8] Lenin did regret the anarchic violence of the masses – not because it was violent but because it was anarchic. As Lenin expressed it a year or so later, a revolutionary Social Democrat should never indulge in 'hackneyed, philistine, petty-bourgeois moralizing' about violence. The proper response was rather to transform 'aimless, senseless, sporadic acts of violence into purposeful, mass violence'.[9]

The basic premise of Lenin's scenario had always been the claim that the capitalist transformation of Russia was calling forth spirits from the *vasty deep* of the people, spirits powerful enough to topple the tsar. The revolution of 1905 showed that these spirits had indeed come when they were called. It was therefore a vindication of Lenin's 'other way' to achieve the dreams of his brother Alexander:

Is it good that the *narod* should apply unlawful, irregular, unmethodical and unsystematic methods of struggle such as seizing their freedom and creating a new, formally unrecognized and revolutionary authority, that it should use force against the oppressors of the *narod*? Yes, it is very good. It is the supreme manifestation of the *narod*'s struggle for freedom. It marks that great period when the dreams of freedom cherished by the best men and women of Russia are translated into *practice*, when freedom becomes the practice of the vast masses of the *narod*, and not merely of individual heroes.[10]

The Role of the Peasant in Lenin's Heroic Scenario

Looking back at the Bolsheviks through the lens of post-1917 events, particularly Stalin's disastrous collectivization and its consequences, we tend to assume that Bolshevism was organically anti-peasant. Yet at the time of the 1905 revolution an informed outside observer praised the Bolsheviks precisely because they were they were 'the popular faction', in contrast to the Mensheviks and their 'attitude of suspicion toward the peasantry'.

The American socialist William Walling travelled through Russia in 1905–7 with his wife Anna Strunsky who was of Russian origin. He met and interviewed many notable figures on both sides of the barricades, including Lenin himself. When he returned he wrote a long, enthusiastic book, still worth reading, entitled *Russia's Message: The True World Import of the Revolution*. Walling's 1908 testimony is all the more intriguing because he later became a violent opponent of the Bolshevik revolution and in 1920 wrote an informed diatribe against it, also worth reading.[11]

Walling was a declared supporter of peasant socialism and regarded the Socialist Revolutionaries (SRs) as the fundamental Russian socialist party. For just this reason he much preferred the Bolsheviks to the Mensheviks. The Bolsheviks, he told his American readers, were 'the progressive and more Russian part' of the Social Democratic party. According to Walling, the Bolshevik acceptance of a peasant alliance reflected the real attitude of the workers themselves, who had little sense of class exclusiveness and wanted to fight together with the 'little bourgeoisie' of town and country. 'The majority faction [= the Bolsheviks] realizes thoroughly the necessity of a full unity in the revolutionary movement.' Walling did take note of the feeling, widespread among all Social Democrats, that 'in the general movement, the working people should have the leading role'. Walling found this to be 'a very wrong attitude, since the peasants in Russia are five times more numerous than all other working classes'.[12]

In his brief account of his interview with Lenin Walling made clear that he did not like Lenin's forecast that the peasant bourgeoisie would inevitably become a class enemy in the future. He was nevertheless impressed by Lenin's 'very full knowledge of the economic and political situation of other countries' and found him to be 'far more open-minded [about the peasants] than the leaders formerly in control of the party'. According to Walling, Lenin was at this time 'perhaps the most popular leader in Russia'.[13]

Lenin's scenario of the peasant in revolution was extremely important to him personally. At the end of 1907 he set it all down in one of his most important if overlooked books, *The Agrarian Programme of Social Democracy in the First Russian Revolution, 1905–1907*, a substantial volume of over 200 pages. This book is the fourth and last in the series of full-scale expositions of his heroic scenario (the first three being *Friends of the People*, 1894, *Development of Capitalism in Russia*, 1899, and *To the Village Poor*, 1903). Lenin took it hard when the tsarist government suppressed its publication. His close comrade Lev Kamenev describes the book's fate in words that undoubtedly expressed Lenin's own attitude: 'The huge manuscript, the fruits of long and persistent labour, the result of a work attempted by no one else, lies for ten years, until 1917, in the bottom of Ilich's trunk. It travels with him from Finland to Geneva, from Paris to Krakow, and after ten years,

'Typical Peasant Members of the Second Duma. Extreme Revolutionists from the Heart of Russia', from William Walling's *Russia's Message* (1908).

is borne back to Petersburg on the waves of the victorious revolution, and so, at last, finds a printer.'[14] When revolution broke out in Russia in 1917, almost Lenin's first thought was: now I can publish my book![15]

The following scenario can be extracted from the dense argument of Lenin's book. If the urban workers were class leaders, then the peasants were class followers. Lenin completely accepted the general Marxist idea that the peasants, scattered in isolated rural villages, could be politically effective only if they accepted the leadership of the more advanced urban classes – either the bourgeoisie or the proletariat. But his insistence on the peasant as follower did not exclude an exalted, even romantic view of the peasant in the revolution. Heroic leaders require heroic followers.

As we have seen, Lenin believed that capitalism was splitting the Russian peasantry into two groups, proto-proletarian and proto-bourgeois. Although this division would be vital for the future socialist revolution it was not so crucial in the case of the people's revolution against the tsar. In this revolution, the peasantry *as a whole* would follow the lead of the proletariat in a crusade against

'Baron Taube and pictures he sent his fiancée to show how he dealt with the peasants . . . These pictures were produced before the First Duma and caused a great sensation', from *Russia's Message* (1908).

the tsar. The 'petty-bourgeois' peasant was therefore still a crucial part of the revolutionary army. Indeed, the most remarkable feature of Lenin's 1907 book *Agrarian Programme* is his enthusiasm about the revolutionary fervour of the petty-bourgeois peasant.

From 1902 the peasants had revealed themselves as effective fighters for the democratic transformation of Russia. The peasants were ready, not only to take the land of the noble estate-owners but, in so doing, to destroy the social base of the tsarist system. And this act of economic liberation would have radical political consequences: 'The peasantry cannot carry out an agrarian revolution without abolishing the old regime, the standing army and the bureaucracy, because all these are the most reliable mainstays of the landed property of the *pomeshchiki* [gentry estate-owners], bound to this system by thousands of ties.'[16] By abolishing the old regime Russia would become a 'peasant republic', and this would be good for the peasants, good for the workers' class struggle and good for Russia.

More unexpectedly, Lenin is also extremely enthusiastic about the 'petty-bourgeois' peasant as an agent of the capitalist transformation of Russia. Freedom would allow the enterprising peasant to evolve into a *fermer* (farmer) – a foreign-sounding word that evoked the enticing model of the progressive and dynamic capitalist farmer that Lenin associated with the United States in particular:

A free mass of farmers may serve as a basis for the development of capitalism without any need whatsoever of *pomeshchik* enterprise . . . Capitalist development along such a path *should* proceed far more broadly, freely, and swiftly owing to the tremendous growth of the home market and an upsurge in the standard of living, the energy, initiative and culture of the *entire* population.[17]

A basic premise of Lenin's heroic scenario was that capitalist transformation of Russia was absolutely inevitable. But Russia was still faced with a tremendously important choice: what *kind* of capitalist transformation? Peasant-based capitalist transformation was not the only possible scenario – in fact, the tsarist government was trying its hardest to set up a much more repressive gentry-based capitalism (as Lenin interpreted the aim of the so-called Stolypin reforms). Gentry-based capitalism was the 'Prussian path' to capitalism, while peasant-based democratic capitalism was the 'American path'. Lenin urged Social Democrats to fight for the American path, even though this path required 'what, from the standpoint of the philistine, or of the philistine historian, are very unusual and "optimistic" assumptions; it requires tremendous peasant initiative, revolutionary energy, purposiveness, organization, and a wealth of creative activity by the *narod*'.[18] This last remark expresses the very heart of Lenin's outlook: rejection of 'philistine' scepticism in favour of an 'optimistic' romanticism about the 'creative activity of the *narod*'.

Ebb-tide of Revolution

The ebbing of the revolutionary tide was dramatically reflected in the fates of the Social Democratic representatives in the Second Duma in 1907. The police had prepared a list of charges against the Duma members that also reads like a bill of indictment against the revolution itself:

> In 1907, in the city of St Petersburg under the name of the Social Democratic Duma delegation, the accused formed a criminal society, the aim of whose activity is the violent over-throw, by means of an armed popular uprising, of the form of government established by the Basic Laws, the removal of the sovereign Emperor from supreme authority and the constitution of a democratic republic in Russia.[19]

Among the specific charges were 'relations with secret criminal societies calling themselves the Central and Petersburg Committees of the RSDWP'; attempts to organize peasants, workers and soldiers into secret associations and to connect up these groups up among themselves; giving inflammatory speeches to illegal gatherings of workers; and providing false passports for people eluding police supervision.[20] All these charges were true, of course. The government demanded that the Duma revoke the legal immunity of its Social Democratic members. The Duma refused and found itself revoked, that is, disbanded and replaced by a new legislature by means of Stolypin's *coup d'état* of 3 June 1907. This date can be taken as the end of the revolutionary period, since the restrictive suffrage and the repressive policies of the 'third of June system' forced most party activity back underground.

The next few years were dismal ones for the party underground. Based on informer reports, a top official in the tsarist political police, Aleksandr Spiridovich, summed up the woes of the underground: 'Systematic arrest of party activists, indifference on the part of workers toward the revolutionary work that had just recently been so popular, mass flight of the intelligentsia that joined forces with the party during the years of revolutionary upsurge, a lack of the financial means that had flowed so plentifully into party coffers not so long ago – all of this meant that local organizations fell apart.'[21]

Spiridovich modestly left out another huge problem facing the underground, one that represented a signal accomplishment of the political police: 'provocation', the infiltration of underground organizations by police informers. The resulting atmosphere was described in 1911 by Bolshevik Gregor Alexinsky, one of the Social Democratic Duma delegates sentenced to hard labour. After escaping to Europe, he observed from afar the effects of the 'treason' committed by disillusioned *praktiki*: 'Then [after 1907] commenced a period which in all truth saw "brother turned against brother", when the breath of treachery poisoned the atmosphere of the revolutionary organizations, and provocation acquired so extraordinary a power that a mutual distrust eventually seized upon all their members. The dismemberment of the organizations followed.'[22]

Having left Russia at the end of 1907, Lenin was again in exile. He and Krupskaya lived in Geneva for another year and moved to Paris at the end of 1908. But wherever his residence, Lenin lived the intense but self-absorbed life of the party intellectual: engaging in endless polemics with factional opponents, preparing resolutions for party congresses, and then arguing about the proper interpretation of official party decisions. These intra-party fights easily degenerated into the squabbles that Russians describe with the

Lenin's apartment at 4, rue Marie-Rose, Paris, 1909–12.

eloquent word *skloki* – the insupportably petty and demeaning infighting that sucked up the time and energy of the émigrés. Krupskaya tells us that Lenin was made physically ill by the atmosphere created by *skloki*. Yet, from the point of view of his opponents, Lenin himself was no mean hand at infighting and hard-line factionalism.

Lenin's life during these years can be – and most often is – described solely in terms of party factional struggles. Some biographers portray Lenin as compulsively seeking exclusive party leadership for himself, by fair means or foul. Others portray him as defending the correct party line against all deviations, whether from the right or the left. In either case the biographical landmarks are the same: a succession of party congresses and conferences, of polemical books and articles, of various campaigns against 'organizational opportunism', 'liquidationism', 'recallism' and similar heresies, seemingly without number.

But Lenin had an inner political life as well, one that lifted him above the day-to-day *skloki* and factional clashes. This was the life of his heroic scenario through which he interpreted events. Thus Lenin's heroic scenario became the emotional link between the enforced smallness of his life and the largeness of the political events of the day. The obsessive factional *skloki* of émigré life acquired meaning because Lenin saw himself as facilitating the emergence of the vast energies of the people. Lenin wanted to inspire the activist to inspire the proletariat to inspire the *narod* to rise up against the tsar, thus giving the whole world another inspiring example of how to carry out a people's revolution.

Lenin's political positions in the intra-party factional infighting followed from his commitment to his heroic scenario. He first insisted that the Social Democrats should keep their eyes on the prize and not retreat from their ambitious goal. This goal was 'democratic revolution to the end', and that meant *full* political freedom. The result – a paradoxical one from our present-day vantage-point – was that the Bolsheviks criticized the Mensheviks for cravenly accepting the few thin slices of political freedom available in Stolypin's Russia rather than demanding the full loaf.

The Mensheviks proposed that the workers focus on attainable goals, for example, achieving a crucial political freedom such as freedom of association. The Bolsheviks agreed that freedom of association was indeed crucial, but insisted that it meant nothing in isolation. As the Bolshevik Lev Kamenev put the case, 'A Marxist should say to the worker masses who have learned from experience the need for freedom of association: freedom to strike, freedom of unions – these are empty words in the absence of inviolability of person, freedom of speech, or freedom of the press. Freedom of association is tied to the basic and fundamental conditions of the country.'[23]

Kamenev's words need to be decoded, since he was writing at a time (1913) when the Bolsheviks had access to legal publication. He therefore resorted to Aesopian language meant to get past the censor. 'Marxist' stood in for 'Social Democrat', and the phrase 'basic and fundamental conditions of the country' pointed to the need for revolution. Kamenev's real message was that there was only one way to get secure freedom of association: a full-scale, revolutionary assault on tsarism in order to introduce the full gamut of political freedoms.

As before, the only way to achieve this ambitious goal was through a vast people's revolution. Menshevik attempts to find allies among the elite liberal bourgeoisie were doomed to failure, since the liberals mortally feared 'the revolutionary whirlwind' and would therefore always stop short and sell out the revolution. Daunting as the task seemed, proletarian leadership of the *narod* was the only way to carry out revolution 'to the end': 'A peasant revolution under the leadership of the proletariat in a capitalist country is difficult, very difficult, but it is possible, and we must fight for it. Three years of the revolution have taught us and the whole *narod* not only that we must fight for it but also how to fight for it.'[24]

Given his ambitious ends (full political freedom) and ambitious means (peasant revolution), Lenin furiously rejected any 'philistine' pessimism. He was especially outraged at Menshevik scepticism about the utility of the uprising of December 1905, given its bloody suppression, as encapsulated by a famous comment by Plekhanov: 'the workers should not have taken up arms'. Lenin's reaction: 'What an ocean of renegade comment was called forth by that assessment!' The proper response from non-philistine Social Democrats must instead be to proclaim openly, for all to hear, for the sake of the wavering and feeble in spirit, to shame those who are turning renegade and deserting socialism, that the workers' party sees in the direct revolutionary struggle of the masses, in the October and December struggles of 1905, the greatest movements of the proletariat since the [Paris] Commune [of 1871].[25]

Looking ahead, Social Democrats must retain their confidence that

the very *first* fresh breeze of freedom, the slightest relaxation of repression, will again *inevitably* call into being hundreds and thousands of organizations, unions, groups, circles and undertakings of a revolutionary-democratic nature. And this will as inevitably result in another 'whirlwind', in a repetition of the October-December struggle, but on an immeasurably greater scale.[26]

The imperative of spreading the good news of socialism and revolution had always been at the heart of Lenin's scenario. The eagerly awaited repetition of 1905 gave this imperative even more urgency. Most of Lenin's factional infighting during the years 1908–12 revolved around this issue. As opposed to the right wing of Social Democracy, he fought against attempts to 'liquidate' the *konspiratsiia* underground. As opposed to the left wing, he fought against the rejection of newly available channels of dissemination, in particular the 'Duma word', the forum provided by the elected legislature to Social Democratic deputies.[27]

Lenin acknowledged that the Social Democratic underground was at present in a state of 'deep collapse', yet he remained fiercely loyal to it as an institution. In a tone of puzzlement, the American historian Leopold Haimson wonders why the Bolsheviks attached such importance during these years to 'issuing pamphlets with their

EXTREME RIGHT

Liquidators: Come close to [non-political] cultural work. Completely disown the underground.

RIGHT

Golosovtsy: [Martov and others grouped around the newspaper *Golos Sotsial-Democrata*]: Tend toward opportunism. Acknowledge both legal and illegal work, but their centre of gravity is in the former.

CENTRE

Plekhanovists: As long as there exist no important differences in principle, accept a bloc with the Bolsheviks. Acknowledge both legal and illegal work, but their centre of gravity is the latter.

Menshevik-Conciliators or Trotskyists: Aim at uniting all party tendencies without exception, acknowledge the necessity of the underground. Acknowledge both legal and illegal work, but their centre of gravity is the latter.

Bolshevik-Conciliators: Represent pure Bolshevism. Aim at uniting all party tendencies that acknowledge that underground work is obligatory. Differ from Trotskyites in that they are 'beki'.

EXTREME LEFT

Vperedists [Bogdanov and others grouped around the newspaper *Vpered*]: Bolsheviks of a radicalist [sic] tendency. Same as the conciliators: center of gravity in the underground.

Leninists: Represent pure Bolshevism. 'Liquidators of the left.'

A police spy's chart of factions within Russian Social Democracy, 1911.

signature and stamp' and to convening 'almost illusory' provisional and regional conferences of underground organizations. 'The reports of the Department of Police paint a pitiful picture of these meetings, usually attended by only a handful of haphazardly elected and self-appointed delegates, including agents of the Okhrana [tsarist political police].'[28]

Lenin's attachment to the *konspiratsiia* underground becomes understandable when we remember the role it plays in his heroic scenario. The *konspiratsiia* underground was the one place in Russia where the Social Democratic message could be proclaimed boldly and uncompromisingly, the one place where the banner of socialism and the democratic republic could be proudly unfurled. This could not happen in any organization that was legally permitted in Stolypin's Russia. Furthermore, the miracle of 1905 showed that, even under tsarism, an underground party could be built that was 'really capable of leading *classes*. In the spring of 1905 our party was a league of underground groups; in the autumn it became the party of *millions* of the proletariat. Do you think, my dear sirs, this came all of a sudden, or was the result *prepared* and secured by years and years of slow, obstinate, inconspicuous, noiseless work?'[29]

Lenin's vision of the *konspiratsiia* underground and its threads strategy remained essentially the same as before 1905. As he described it in 1908, 'this illegal core will spread *its* feelers, *its* influence, incomparably wider than before'. But since the intelligentsia as a whole was losing interest in socialism and revolution, the 'revolutionaries by trade' who kept the underground up and running had to be recruited predominantly from 'advanced members from among the workers themselves'.[30] Despite all the problems faced by the underground, Lenin was confident that the pamphlets issued by the Bolsheviks were a seed that '*has been sown* ... And this seed will bear its fruits – perhaps not tomorrow or the day after but a little later; we cannot alter the objective conditions in which a new crisis is growing – but it will bear fruit.'[31]

Lenin's emotional intensity about the need to get the word out also revealed itself in attacks on those of his fellow Bolsheviks who (as it seemed to him) neglected the value of 'the Duma word'. His feelings are evident in a verbal video of Lenin in his underwear found in the memoirs of Georgy Solomon, a long-time Bolshevik who later occupied a high position as a Soviet trade representative. In 1923 Solomon grew so disgusted with the mores of the Soviet government that he stayed abroad. The following scene is taken from memoirs published in Paris around 1930.

In 1908 Solomon lived in Brussels and hosted Lenin when he visited the Belgian capital. On this occasion Lenin was in town to give a talk on the current situation. The speech did not go over very well, in Solomon's opinion. Lenin vainly tried 'to inspire those who gloomily doubted by insisting that the revolutionary movement had not died away but was proceeding forward at its own pace'.[32] After the speech they retired to Solomon's apartment and talked politics. It was after midnight, and both men had got ready for bed. Solomon was already in bed while Lenin, in his usual style, paced up and down making his points – this time in his underwear. The conversation moved on to the problems of the Social Democratic deputies. Solomon was a 'recallist', that is, he wanted to force the Social Democratic delegation of the Duma to resign. Recallism did not arise from an anti-parliamentary bias – on the contrary, the heart of the Bolshevik revolutionary program at this time was to bring a 'bourgeois democratic' parliament to Russia. Nor did the recallists refuse in principle to participate in such a pitiful excuse for a parliament as the current Duma. Solomon and other recallists simply felt that the mediocrities now fumbling around in the Duma chamber in the name of Social Democracy were not 'tribunes of the people' but simply an embarrassment.

Lenin got angrier and angrier at Solomon's stand. Supporting the Social Democratic deputies wasn't softness on the part of the

'Social Democratic Deputies in the First Duma', from *Russia's Message* (1908).

current party leadership, Lenin exclaimed, 'but simply a desire
to preserve our parliamentary group, as is advantageous to a
party that stands at the head of the proletariat and expresses its
revolutionary interests. And anybody whose brain isn't completely
clouded over should realize this.' Solomon retorted (in a calm and
business-like fashion, he tells us) that the current incumbents were
so incompetent that they even threatened to damage the prestige
of the Russian Social Democrats in the eyes of European socialists.
Lenin exploded:

> Oh, that's it! That means, we should recall them. A very clever
> solution that does great honour to the profundity and political
> wisdom of those who thought it up! Let me tell you, my very
> good and most excellent sir, that 'recallism' is not a mistake –
> it's a crime! Everything in Russia is now asleep, everything has
> died away in some sort of Oblomov-style dream. Stolypin stifles
> everything, the atmosphere of reaction becomes more and
> more all-embracing. And now, in the words of M. K. Tsebrikova
> (I hope you know the name, my very esteemed sir), I remind you

that 'when the dour wave of reaction is about to sweep over and swallow everything that still lives, then all those who represent a progressive outlook are called upon to cry out to those who are losing spirit: Stand firm!' This duty should be clear to anyone with half a brain.[33]

And when Lenin realized that Solomon thought that having no Social Democratic presence in the Duma was preferable to the current situation, he indignantly interrupted: 'What?! According to you, it's better to let the Duma go on without any of our representatives at all?! Well, only political cretins and brainless idiots, out-and-out reactionaries, could think like that.'

At this point Solomon protested against what he considered personal attacks. Lenin backtracked, gave him a sort of hug, and assured him that the expressions that escaped him in the heat of argument were not meant to be taken personally – and perhaps they weren't! (Similar apologies can be found throughout Lenin's correspondence.) Lenin's curiously impersonal abuse was not directed at Solomon as an individual, but against all the sceptics, pessimists, defeatists – in a word, philistines – who refused to lift themselves up to the grand vistas of his heroic scenario.

The 'Commencing Revolution'

The differences among the Social Democrats were so sharp that the question more and more became: two parties or one? That is, were the various tactical and organizational differences among Social Democrats so great as to force a split? Many of the *praktiki* and the rank-and-file party members in Russia thought not, thus putting heavy pressure on the émigrés to work out a modus vivendi. But the upshot was that the party's orientation veered back and forth as one or another faction gained control or, just as bad, the central

A formal portrait of Lenin in 1910, when he was living in Paris. Here he presents a respectable middle-class front, very unlike his image after the Revolution.

institutions got bogged down into an enforced *immobilisme*. At one point in the TV series *Buffy the Vampire Slayer* a demon goddess and a normal human are forced to share the same body, each taking over at unexpected moments, each destroying the continuity of the other one's life, each finding themselves in unexpected and embarrassing circumstances. The Russian Social Democratic party faced a similar situation.

Lenin's stand can be guessed from the title of a book he had Kamenev write in 1911: *Two Parties*.[34] The argument of this book was that two parties existed de facto, and productive work would be impossible until they had a separate existence de jure. Lenin wanted to purify the party by pushing the Menshevik 'liquidators' out of

Lenin and Grigory Zinoviev hiking near Zakopane, Poland, in the summer of 1913.

the party and, to prove his bona fides, he did his best to push the Bolshevik 'recallists' out in the same way. Following a familiar logic the 'conciliators' within the party, the ones who wanted everybody to get along and therefore condemned any split, were also condemned.

By 1912 Lenin had decided to cut the knot of Damocles by simply deciding that his group was the real party. After a series of institutional manoeuvres the so-called Prague Conference of January 1912 – consisting of Lenin, Zinoviev and about fourteen Bolshevik *praktiki* from Russia – elected a new Central Committee and thus a new party. Shortly after the Prague Conference Lenin and Krupskaya, accompanied by Zinoviev and his family, moved from Paris to Krakow in the Austrian section of Poland. Krakow was closer to Russia than any of Lenin's previous exile locations and communication with Petersburg was relatively easy. The Bolshevik leadership nucleus considered this only a semi-exile.

Lenin's change of residence coincided with a new mood in Russia – an upsurge of disaffection and militancy. The shooting down of striking workers in the gold-mines of Lena in Siberia was the mini-Bloody Sunday that crystallized the growing impatience. The Lena massacre on 17 April 1912 outraged all of Russian society; in particular, it sparked off a round of worker protests and strikes. The new worker militancy meant increased support for the Bolsheviks in the factional struggle and Lenin could now claim solid majority support in aboveground organizations such as trade unions and cooperative societies. The new Bolshevik aboveground presence was symbolized by the launch of a legal newspaper that later became world famous. The first issue of *Pravda* came out on 5 May 1912.

Lenin ended the second decade of his political career in much the same sort of situation as he began it, dangerously isolated in the world of international socialism but enjoying a solid base of support within the party back in Russia. The other émigré leaders of Russian Social Democracy did not agree on much, but they were all genuinely repulsed by what they saw as Lenin's hard-line approach and arrogant splitting tactics. Just a little while earlier, Plekhanov had been a de facto ally of Lenin in the fight against 'liquidationism'. But now even Plekhanov denounced Lenin's unilateral election of a new Central Committee as an attempt to use for factional advantage party funds he had acquired by various crooked methods (arguments over party funds and Lenin's methods in obtaining control over them had been going on for years). The exasperation of Russian party leaders with Lenin communicated itself to Western European socialists who felt called upon to try and make peace among the squabbling Russians. In July 1914 European socialist leaders met in Brussels in order to sort out these problems. Lenin's representative, Inessa Armand, took an uncompromising stand, and probably only the outbreak of war later that summer saved Lenin from condemnation and complete isolation.

In contrast the Bolsheviks back home in Russia were gaining influence, giving Lenin a solid base to support his intransigence.

Roman Malinovsky,
Bolshevik Central
Committee member
and police spy.

Lenin constantly quoted statistics based on newspaper circulation and worker donations to back up his claim that the Bolsheviks were now the real representatives of the Russian worker movement. His typical optimism about the trend of events found expression in the instructions he sent Inessa Armand on how to present the Bolshevik case at the Brussels conference. If someone objected that the Bolsheviks had only a small majority within a certain section of the Russian party, he told her, she should answer 'yes, it is small. If you like to wait, it will soon be *écrasante*'.[35]

The short slice of time between the Prague Conference of January 1912 and the outbreak of world war in August 1914 presents us with two of the greatest personal mysteries of Lenin's career: Roman Malinovsky and Inessa Armand. Knowledge of Lenin's heroic scenario allows us to shed at least some light on these mysteries. My discussion is limited to this aspect.

Malinovsky was a genuine man of the people who became prominent in the union movement after 1905 and was wooed by both Social Democratic factions as a candidate for the Fourth Duma that was elected in 1912. He joined up with the Bolsheviks and promptly became a real star. His eloquent speeches in the Duma effectively used the parliamentary tribune that was one of the very few legal channels for agitation open to the Social Democrats. But in actuality Malinovsky was on the payroll of the tsarist political police. Most people correctly deduced that he was an informer when in 1914 he suddenly and without explanation resigned from the Duma and fled the country. But Lenin doggedly defended Malinovsky's innocence and viciously attacked anyone who suggested otherwise. Only after the fall of tsarism in 1917 was he forced to face the truth.

How did Lenin manage to deceive himself so thoroughly? In Lenin's eyes Malinovsky was a 'Russian Bebel', that is, an outstanding party leader of worker origin. He played to perfection a central role in Lenin's heroic scenario: the 'purposive worker' who, inspired by Social Democratic teaching about the mission of the proletariat, was able to inspire others in turn. We have seen how Lenin in *What Is to Be Done?* dreamed of an ideal party activist who could 'merge in himself a knowledge of the worker milieu [with] a freshness of socialist conviction', who could 'rely on the boundless confidence of the broadest worker mass' because he himself was boundlessly devoted to the revolution.[36] A party populated by Malinovskys would be invincible. No wonder Lenin refused to accept that Malinovsky was a paid actor and not the real thing.

Certainly the 'purposive worker' was far from being just a myth – in fact, Malinovsky himself was not a complete fake. He was just a spectacular reminder that real life never seems to confirm our narratives without slipping in an ironic twist.

Inessa Armand in internal exile, photographed with fellow exiles, 1908.

The daughter of a French opera singer and an English actress, Inessa Armand was an unlikely Bolshevik. Born in Paris, she grew up in Moscow and married the son of a wealthy manufacturer. She and her husband opened a school for peasant children, an activity that later might have constituted a link with Lenin and Krupskaya. After an amicable separation from her husband she became more deeply involved in the Social Democratic underground and was arrested in 1907. She escaped from internal exile and ended up in Paris, where she met Lenin.

Long before Armand's death in 1920 rumours were circulating about a romantic link between her and Lenin. Many historians believe that recently published correspondence between the two has clinched the case for the existence of an affair. But the evidence is still circumstantial and scepticism on this point is still legitimate. For my part, after reading through the relevant documents from Lenin, Armand and Krupskaya, I find it hard to believe that Lenin and Armand had an adulterous affair.

Armand's role in Lenin's life should not be reduced to her alleged stint as 'Lenin's mistress'. As a trusted confidante – possibly the only woman outside his family to be part of his inner circle – Armand had full opportunity to see all sides of Lenin's character. She often had to bear the brunt of his factional infighting. Lenin sent her to represent the Bolsheviks at the 1914 conference in Brussels, where she had to defend an unpopular and marginalized standpoint. Lenin thanked her profusely, saying that he himself would have exploded in anger.[37]

But Inessa Armand was also in a position to see Lenin's determined optimism at close range. In late 1911 the prominent French socialists Paul and Laura Lafargue (Laura was one of Karl Marx's daughters) committed double suicide because they felt they could no longer be of use to the cause. Lenin spoke at their funeral in Paris, and Armand translated his remarks into French:

We can now see with particular clarity how rapidly we are nearing the triumph of the cause to which Lafargue devoted all his life. The Russian revolution ushered in an era of democratic revolutions throughout Asia, and 800 million people are now joining the democratic movement of the whole of the civilized world. In Europe, peaceful bourgeois parliamentarianism is drawing to an end, to give place to an era of revolutionary battles by a proletariat that has been organized and educated in the spirit of Marxist ideas, and that will overthrow bourgeois rule and establish a communist system.[38]

Lenin's sanguine view of world developments was matched by his excitement about the relative upsurge of 1912–14 in Russia that he saw as the beginning of the bigger and better 1905 he had long been awaiting. His description of May Day strikes and demonstrations in Petersburg in 1913 shows his excitement at the thought that his heroic scenario of class leadership was once again being realized in action. As in the mid-1890s Lenin's emphasis is on the power of the Social Democratic message to move the masses into action, even when transmitted by small and inadequate technical means. He therefore claimed that although the Social Democratic message in 1913 may have originated in a very small group in Petersburg, its impact was felt all over Russia in ever-widening circles. In response to Menshevik scepticism he described the course of the demonstrations of May 1913 in the following way.

The St Petersburg underground consisted of several hundred workers who were nevertheless (as Lenin writes in 'May Day Action by the Revolutionary Proletariat', 1913) 'the flower of the St Petersburg proletariat . . . esteemed and appreciated by the *entire* working class of Russia'. They issue some hasty, poorly printed, and unattractive looking pamphlets. 'And lo, a miracle!' – a quarter of a million workers rise up 'as one man' in strikes and demonstrations in Petersburg. 'Singing revolutionary songs, with loud calls for revolution, in all suburbs of the capital and from one end of the city to another, with red banners waving, the worker crowds fought over the course of several hours against the police and the Okhrana [security police] that had been mobilized with extraordinary energy by the government.'

The leaflets and the revolutionary speeches by workers carry the message that a revolution to install the democratic republic is the only way to ensure freedom. This message does not stop at the city limits of Petersburg. The industrial proletariat is able to 'draw into revolutionary actions the labouring and exploited masses, deprived of basic rights and driven into a desperate situation'. The revolutionary strikes of the Russian proletariat – the mighty weapon it forged for itself in 1905 – are therefore 'stirring, rousing, enlightening, and organizing the masses of the *narod* for revolution'. In fact, the May Day strikes and demonstrations will show 'to the whole world that the Russian proletariat is steadfastly following its revolutionary course'.

Thus, in Lenin's exalted view, the small Social Democratic underground of Petersburg sent a message heard around the world. And why? – because it told the truth to millions about their hopeless position under tsarism, thus 'inspiring them with faith in revolutionary struggle'.[39]

In 1914, on the eve of war, Lenin wrote to Inessa Armand (in English), 'Best greetings for the commencing revolution in Russia'.[40] A new 'era of revolutionary battles' was indeed commencing, and not only in Russia. During the next five years, his heroic scenario would be vindicated on a global scale – or so it seemed to Lenin.

For many Marxists, a purely democratic revolution could be 'only' a bourgeois revolution – a necessary step forward, but a frustrating one, since it ushered in a long period of bourgeois class domination. Confining oneself to working for the bourgeois revolution while deferring the socialist revolution was an eminently reasonable self-limitation, but nevertheless it was an emotionally difficult substitute for the real thing. Lenin also accepted completely that the 1905 revolution was no more than a bourgeois, political, democratic one and that its historical meaning was limited to clearing the path for socialist revolution. But emotionally there was for him nothing 'only' about the events of 1905. He saw them as a vast national epic – a heroic struggle of the *narod* to conquer freedom and to regenerate Russia.

As usual, Lenin's emotional commitment to an exalted view of events spills out in ceaseless polemics with all those he considered philistines, pedants, whiners, sceptics, defeatists. Did the slowdown in the strike movement in 1904 mean that the proletariat was no longer interested in revolution? No, the proletariat was merely biding its time. Was the disorder and violent chaos of the revolution in 1905 a bad thing? No, it was a good thing, an explosion of popular creativity. Was the Moscow uprising of December 1905, drowned in the blood of the workers, a mistake committed by over-enthusiastic socialist activists? No, it represented the most splendid popular movement since the Paris Commune of 1871. Were the peasants who burned down landowner estates while dreaming of equalized land tenure a backward and reactionary class capable only of spontaneous outbursts of violence? No, the 'petty-bourgeois peasants' were a progressive class that was fighting for a democratic form of capitalism, and therefore a worthy ally of the Russian proletariat in the democratic revolution. Did the new political institutions created by the revolution mean that the previous *konspiratsiia* underground had become anachronistic, an embarrassing relic that ought to be liquidated? No, the old underground had sown the seeds that had burst forth in the glory of the 1905 revolution. The underground therefore had to be preserved in the post-revolutionary era in order to prepare for the inevitable replay of a bigger and better 1905, when 'the Russian WORKER, elevated to the head of all democratic elements, will overthrow absolutism'.

4

Three Train Rides

'A new era of revolutions is drawing near.'
Karl Kautsky, 1909, as paraphrased by Lenin, 1914

Krakow to Bern

In the early summer of 1914 Lenin had very little idea of
what the looming war would bring. He even assumed his
workload would be eased somewhat if war actually broke out,
since his connections with the Russian underground would be
thoroughly disrupted.[1] But when war did come it brought some
devastating surprises.

Even after Germany declared war on Russia on 1 August 1914,
the Social Democratic parties in Germany, Austro-Hungary and
France were still organizing mass protests against war. The main
German party newspaper, *Vorwärts*, continued to thunder against
the imperialist war and to threaten the capitalist warmongers with
revolutionary action. But on 5 August Lenin received a major shock:
the SPD Reichstag delegation had voted unanimously for war credits.
Forgotten was the traditional cry of 'not one penny – not one man'
for the capitalist state. When Lenin first saw the headlines in the
village of Poronino (his summer residence outside Krakow, which
he used after moving back to Poland in 1912), he was sure that
they must be a provocation, a trick by the government to confuse
the opposition.

Lenin after his
release from jail
in Nowy Targ,
Galicia, August
1914.

Lenin soon had his own firsthand experience with war hysteria.
The local officials in Austrian Poland suspected the outlandish
Russian emigrant of espionage. A policeman reported to his
superiors that many meetings of Russian nationals had taken
place at the residence of V. Ulyanov. There were rumours that
Ulyanov had been seen taking photographs in the surrounding
hills, but these proved unfounded. Nevertheless, the policeman was
of the opinion that Ulyanov should be under lock and key – after
all, his identity papers were in French (the language of an enemy
country), he received money from Petersburg, and he was in a very
good position to give information about Austria to the Russians.[2]

Based on this irrefutable logic, Lenin was arrested and kept
in the local jail from 8 to 19 August. Thus the third decade of his
political career began the same way as his first decade – in jail.

And, as in Siberian exile, Lenin devoted some of his time to helping peasants with their legal troubles, only this time the peasants were his fellow jail mates. But the big difference between 1895 and 1914 was that Lenin now had powerful friends on the outside. Among these was the leader of the Austrian Social Democrats, Victor Adler, who went to the Austrian Minister of the Interior to give personal assurance that no one was less likely to help the tsarist government than V. Ulyanov. When the minister asked, 'are you sure he's an enemy of the tsar?' Adler answered, 'he is a more implacable enemy than your Excellency'.

Orders soon came down to release Lenin, and even to allow him to travel to Switzerland. On getting out of jail Lenin received another shock, in the form of a leaflet entitled 'Declaration of Russian Socialists Joining the French Army as Volunteers'. These Russian socialists outdid the Germans in their support of their government's war effort: they joined the ranks of an allied army. Among the émigrés in France who showed their devotion to internationalism in this way were several Bolsheviks.

Among many harrowing scenes of wartime hysteria and early military casualties (vividly described by Krupskaya in one of the most gripping sections of her memoirs), Lenin, his wife and his confused and soon-to-die mother-in-law packed up and embarked on a week-long train trip to Bern, Switzerland (with a stop in Vienna to get necessary documents and to thank Victor Adler, soon to be a political enemy). When he arrived in Bern on 5 September Lenin hit the ground running. The day he stepped off the train he met with local Bolshevik émigrés and proposed a set of theses about the proper reaction to the war. Just a month had gone by since the outbreak of hostilities – a month mostly taken up with the hassles and uncertainties of jail and of leaving Poland – and yet Lenin was ready with theses that defined a radically new chapter of his career.

We hardly exaggerate if we say that one Lenin got on the train in Krakow and another Lenin got off in Bern. The Krakow Lenin was a Russian Social Democrat with opinions about European and global issues. The Bern Lenin was a European Social Democrat of Russian origin. Lenin had long been of the opinion that the final episode of his heroic scenario – in the words of his banner sentence of 1894, when the Russian proletariat, side by side with the proletariat of all countries, would take 'the direct road of open political struggle to the victorious communist revolution' – was fast approaching in the countries of Western Europe. But since, as he saw it, the leaders of European Social Democracy had now abandoned the banner of revolutionary socialism, he, Lenin, would stride forward to pick it up.

Central to the programme of this new Lenin was a vision of a world entering an era of revolutions. Western Europe was on the eve of the final, socialist revolution. In Russia the democratic anti-tsarist revolution was already 'commencing' (as Lenin had written to Inessa Armand in summer 1914). All over the world, national and anti-colonial revolutions were brewing. These various genres of revolutions would inevitably influence each other in an intense process of interaction. In Lenin's vision, the world war that broke out in 1914 had tremendously accelerated the process of global interaction. The miseries caused by the imperialist war would speed up revolution everywhere. Any successful revolution – whether socialist, democratic or national – would then spark off revolution in other countries, often by means of revolutionary war. After a socialist revolution, for example, 'the victorious proletariat of that country, after expropriating the capitalists and organizing their own socialist production, will arise *against* the rest of the world – the capitalist world – attracting to its cause the oppressed classes of other countries, stirring uprisings in those countries against the capitalists, and in case of need using even armed force again the exploiting classes and their states'.[3] In this invocation of revolutionary war we easily see Lenin's familiar scenario of inspiring class leadership, now applied on an international scale.

The manifest duty of socialists everywhere was therefore to 'turn the imperialist war into a civil war' – that is, to use the crisis caused by the war in order to accelerate the revolution on a national and international scale. But, as Lenin observed with horror, a large majority of European socialist leaders had reneged on this duty when they supported their own government's war effort. Lenin already believed that 'opportunism' – the deluded hope that socialism could be achieved other than by class revolution – was an insidiously powerful force in the European Social Democratic parties. Majority socialist support for the war convinced him that the rot of opportunism had infected Social Democracy at its core. In a Bolshevik manifesto drafted by Lenin in October 1914 he announced 'with deepest sorrow' that 'the most influential socialist leaders' had 'defamed socialism'. Their conduct inspired 'a burning feeling of shame', because they 'dishonoured the banner' of revolutionary Social Democracy.[4]

According to many writers on Lenin the shock of socialist betrayal in 1914 kicked off a process of rethinking that led to the rejection of what he had earlier considered to be Marxist orthodoxy. According to Lenin himself it was not he who had changed but the others. He insisted that the vision of a world in revolution that I have just outlined was part and parcel of a universal consensus among pre-war revolutionary Marxists. Thus comments such as this one are a constant feature of his wartime rhetoric: 'there is no need here for us to prove that the objective conditions in Western Europe are ripe for a socialist revolution; this was admitted before the war by all influential socialists in all advanced countries'.[5]

Lenin presented himself not as a bold innovator or a fearless rethinker but as someone faithful to the old verities – as the socialist leader who kept his head while all about him were losing theirs. This is how he could walk off the train in Bern in September 1914 and start agitating that very day on the basis of a platform that remained unchanged until the outbreak of the Russian revolution in spring

1917. This is how he had the amazing self-assurance to defy the entire socialist establishment in the name of Marxist orthodoxy.

The emotional content of Lenin's politics during this period cannot be understand without grasping his ferocious anger at the way that socialist leaders reneged *on their own word*. For Lenin one of the most glaring examples of this behaviour – an example he recalled again and again – was the refusal to honour the declaration issued by the Basel International Congress of 1912. There, in solemn conclave assembled, the representatives of European Social Democratic parties had resolved that in the event of war, Social Democrats would 'use the economic and political crisis created by the war to rouse the masses and thereby hasten the downfall of capitalist class rule'.[6]

Lenin had a personal relation to the mandate of the Basel Congress, since he himself, along with Rosa Luxemburg and L. Martov, had been instrumental in adding a similar pledge to a resolution passed by an earlier international socialist congress in 1907. This personal connection was just one more reason why Lenin saw the Basel Manifesto of 1912 as an expression of Social Democratic consensus, as a summary of 'millions and millions of proclamations, newspaper articles, books, speeches of the socialists of all countries' from the entire epoch of the Second International (the international socialist organization that united the main socialist parties from the mid-1890s to 1914). 'To brush aside the Basel Manifesto means to brush aside the whole history of socialism.'[7]

Lenin blamed 'opportunism' for this betrayal and his feelings found expression in an emotional call for purification: 'The European war has done much good to international socialism in that it has disclosed the whole extent of the rottenness, vileness, and meanness in opportunism, and thereby has given a wonderful stimulus for purging the worker movement of the dung which had accumulated during the decades of the peaceful epoch.'[8] Many

European socialists were taken aback by Lenin's purificatory zeal. A French socialist who supported his country's war effort, Solomon Grumbach, no doubt spoke for many:

> In speaking of [Lenin and Zinoviev] we deal with the Grand Inquisitors of the International, who fortunately lack the power of carrying out their ideas, for otherwise Europe would have known many more funeral pyres and quite a few of us would have been seared over a slow fire to the accompaniment of Leninist hymns on the 'only true Leninist socialism' and would have thrown into the hell of socialist traitors as lost filthy-bourgeois-chauvinist-nationalist-social-patriotic souls.[9]

The same reaction of disappointed anger accounts for Lenin's feelings toward the person who was probably the central figure in his emotional life during this period: Karl Kautsky. Lenin read with horror Kautsky's many articles of autumn 1914 in which Kautsky seemed to tie himself in knots, not exactly in order to defend the new opportunism, but to excuse it, to cut it as much slack as possible, to avoid burning bridges within the party. Lenin's consequent obsession with Kautsky was so overwhelming that it puzzled some of his own sympathizers, who knew that Kautsky was rapidly becoming a marginal figure in German socialism. Kautsky became the focus of Lenin's anger because he embodied not only the pre-war Marxist orthodoxy to which Lenin still swore loyalty but also the refusal to live up to that orthodoxy when the chips were down. In letters written in autumn 1914 Lenin vented his feelings. 'Obtain without fail and reread (or ask to have it translated for you) *Road to Power* by Kautsky [and see] what he writes there about the revolution of our time! And now, how he acts the toady and disavows all that! . . . I hate and despise Kautsky now more than anyone, with his vile, dirty, self-satisfied hypocrisy.'[10]

Lenin followed his own advice: he reread Kautsky's 1909 publication *Road to Power* and devoted a whole article to the contrast between what Kautsky wrote there and what he was writing now.[11] Indeed, Lenin took his own vision of global revolution more from Kautsky than from any other writer. As Kautsky wrote in *Road to Power*, 'today, the battles in the liberation struggle of labouring and exploited humanity are being fought not only at the Spree River and the Seine, but also at the Hudson and Mississippi, at the Neva . . . and the Dardanelles, at the Ganges and the Hoangho.'[12] In contrast the wartime Kautsky seemed to Lenin to be an embodiment of philistinism, the age-old enemy of Lenin's heroic scenario, and Lenin's extensive anti-philistine vocabulary peppers every page of his many anti-Kautsky diatribes. Lenin coined a term for this new and insidious form of philistinism: *kautskianstvo*, defined as the use of orthodox phraseology as a cover-up for de facto opportunism. *Kautskianstvo* is usually given the misleading translation 'Kautskyism', but this rendering implies that Lenin is rejecting the system of views propagated by Kautsky before the war. On the contrary the term *kautskianstvo* affirms Lenin's loyalty to Kautsky's pre-war views by violently condemning his 'renegade' behaviour in failing to live up to them. The intensity of Lenin's feelings about Kautsky after 1914 reminds one of a disappointed lover – and perhaps that is the best way to look at it. Lenin hated Kautsky because he loved Kautsky's books.

Immediately upon arriving in Switzerland in September 1914 Lenin moved to get Europe-wide support for his platform. As the anti-war currents in the socialist movement began to get their bearings after the August catastrophe of socialist support for the war, Lenin became the main spokesman for what became known as the Left Zimmerwald movement. The geographic part of this label came from the small resort town 10 kilometres south of Bern, where disaffected socialists from a number of countries came together on 5 September 1915 to discuss aims and strategy.

Few in number as they were, and isolated as they seemed to be from the socialist mainstream, the delegates felt confident that their influence could only grow as the war dragged on.

Lenin's efforts to stake out a position to the left of most Zimmerwald partisans led to the formation of the Left Zimmerwald movement. As opposed to the Zimmerwald majority Lenin wanted no talk of peace as the overriding goal. Only socialist revolution could cut off the capitalist roots of war, and socialist revolution, in the short term, might require more fighting rather than less. Lenin also felt that the Zimmerwald majority was too easy on socialists who supported the war and too sentimental about the possibility of resurrecting the Second International. In private Lenin referred to the Zimmerwald majority as 'Kautskyite shit-heads'.[13] Left Zimmerwald was a minority within a minority but Lenin was unfazed. He was confident that the workers would soon support his stand, no matter how grim things looked at present. In a letter of 1915 Lenin calculated the forces he could count on during the upcoming Zimmerwald conference: 'The Dutch plus ourselves plus the Left Germans plus zero – but that does not matter, it will not be zero afterwards, but *everybody*.'[14]

In early 1916 Lenin and Krupskaya visited Zurich so that Lenin could use the city library to research his book *Imperialism: The Highest Stage of Capitalism* (another work that to a large extent is a defence of Kautsky-then against the apostasy of Kautsky-now). The visit kept being prolonged until the couple decided to stay permanently in Zurich. Here they lived, as Krupskaya recalled, 'a quiet jog-trot life', renting rooms in a shoemaker's flat, attending performances by Russian theatrical companies and picking mushrooms ('Vladimir Ilich suddenly caught sight of some edible mushrooms, and although it was raining, he began to pick them eagerly, as if they were so many Left Zimmerwaldians he were enlisting to our side').[15] Nevertheless, the role of one crying in the wilderness imposed a tremendous strain. Zinoviev recalled in 1918 that many who knew Lenin were surprised how much his appearance had altered under the stress of the war and the collapse of the International.[16]

Despite his engagement with the Left Zimmerwald movement, Lenin did not give up hopes for 'the commencing revolution in Russia', only he saw it more than ever as part of a *global* revolutionary process. As he wrote in October 1915, 'The task of the proletariat in Russia is to carry out the bourgeois democratic revolution in Russia to the end [*do kontsa*], *in order* to ignite the socialist revolution in Europe' [Lenin's emphasis] . . . There is no doubt that a victory of the proletariat in Russia would create extraordinary favourable conditions for the development of revolution both in Asia and in Europe. *Even* 1905 proved that.'[17]

There is a widespread impression that Lenin was growing downhearted and pessimistic about the chance of revolution just weeks before the fall of the tsar in early 1917.[18] In actuality the approach of the Russian revolution during the winter of 1916–17 was visible even to Lenin and his entourage, observing events in far-off Switzerland. In December 1916 Lenin pointed to 'the mounting mass resentment and the strikes and demonstrations that are forcing the Russian bourgeoisie frankly to admit that the revolution is on the march'.[19] In a letter of 10 February 1917 to Inessa Armand Lenin related that his sources in Moscow were optimistic about the revolutionary mood of the workers: 'there will surely be a holiday on our street' (a Russian idiom meaning 'our day will come').[20]

At the end of January 1917 – a few weeks before the February revolution was sparked off by street demonstrations in Petrograd – Lenin's close comrade, Grigory Zinoviev, also observed that 'the revolution is maturing in Russia'. Zinoviev also saw the approaching revolution in Russia through the lens of Lenin's heroic scenario of class leadership. Zinoviev accurately conveyed – though perhaps in more flowery language than Lenin – the emotional fervour behind the Bolshevik scenario:

Oh, if one word of truth – of truth about the war, of truth about the tsar, of truth about the selfish bourgeoisie – could finally reach the blocked Russian village, buried under mountains of snow! Oh, if this word of truth would then penetrate even to the depths of the Russian army that is made up, in its vast majority, of peasants! Then, the heroic working class of Russia, with the support of the poor members of the peasant class, would finally deliver our country from the shame of the monarchy and lead it with a sure hand towards an alliance with the socialist proletariat of the entire world.[21]

Zurich to Petrograd

On 15 March 1917 Lenin learned about the thrilling events in Petrograd (the more Russian-sounding name given to St Petersburg at the beginning of the war): the tsar had abdicated, a government based on Duma representatives had taken power, and workers and soldiers had immediately formed a soviet based on the 1905 model. All Lenin's thoughts now turned to getting to Russia, and since the Allied governments, especially England, had not the slightest intention of helping an anti-war agitator agitate against the war, he accepted the offer of travelling to Russia by means of a sealed train through Germany (most other Russian Social Democrats in Switzerland soon followed by the same route).

The train one which Lenin, Krupskaya, Inessa Armand and about thirty other émigrés travelled was sealed from Gottmadingen station on the German–Swiss border all the way to Sassnitz on Germany's Baltic coast, where the travellers boarded a Swedish ferry. Lenin hoped that the strict rules forbidding contact between the Russian émigrés and any German citizens would minimize the impact of his ride through enemy territory. Although Lenin's dramatic journey in the sealed train has attracted much attention,

Lenin photographed by a journalist while in Stockholm en route to Russia, April 1917. Lenin has yet to adopt the worker's cap he wore following his return to Russia.

in essence it was no different from his train ride in 1914 from Krakow to Bern (true, the 1914 train was not sealed and Lenin was able to stop off in Vienna and thank Victor Adler in person). In each case the government of a country at war with Russia was glad to give safe passage to an enemy national who was a foe of the Russian government. We can also say about the 1917 train trip what we said about the 1914 trip: one man got on the train, another got off. In Switzerland Lenin was a marginal émigré, while in Petrograd he was a respected, even feared, party leader and a factor in national politics. The earlier train-ride from Krakow to Bern in 1914, however, did not mark a boundary in the evolution of Lenin's views – Lenin still adhered to the same view of the world, only more so. In contrast, literally the day before his train left the Zurich station in 1917, Lenin's scenario of class leadership underwent a modification with far-reaching implications.

The so-called 'April Theses' announced by Lenin as soon as he arrived in Petrograd have traditionally been regarded as the expression of a major shift in Lenin's outlook, yet identifying exactly what is new in these theses is quite difficult. The key parts of the April Theses – militant opposition to a government of 'revolutionary chauvinists' intent on continuing the war, all power to the soviets, winning over the peasants by advocating immediate land seizures and diplomacy bent on changing the imperialist war into a civil war – can all be found in a set of theses published in October 1915. Indeed the April Theses might very well be called the October Theses.[22]

In his earlier 1915 theses, and right up to the day before he left Switzerland, Lenin had spoken of two distinct types of revolutions: the democratic revolution in Russia and the socialist revolution in Western Europe. In Lenin's scenario the Russian revolution incites the European revolution, making the two revolutions closely linked but nevertheless separate. Accordingly Lenin never considers the possibility of socialist transformation in Russia prior to and independent of socialist revolution in Europe. The abdication of the tsar did not in itself imply any change in his outlook, since carrying the democratic revolution 'to the end' was still very much on the agenda. Indeed, Lenin's first reaction to the news from Russia was to exult that the theses of October 1915 said 'directly, clearly, exactly, how it will be with us with a revolution in Russia, and they say it one and a half years before the revolution. These theses have been remarkably confirmed, word-for-word, by the revolution.'[23]

Only in an unpublished draft written on 8 April 1917 (Lenin left for Russia on 9 April) do we find for the first time the idea of 'steps toward socialism' *in Russia itself*. The metaphor of 'steps toward socialism' was designedly tentative. Neither at this time nor later did Lenin argue that Russia could achieve full socialism without European revolution. Nevertheless, 'steps toward socialism' represents something new in his outlook. For the first time Lenin suggests that Russia can at least start moving toward socialism without waiting for European revolution. And since we are familiar with Lenin's life-long heroic scenario, we are not surprised to find that Lenin tightly links the idea of 'steps toward socialism' in Russia with proletarian leadership, not of the peasantry as a whole, but of the 'poorest peasantry' who were themselves exploited by capitalism.[24] As we shall see, the link between 'steps toward socialism' and class conflict *within* the peasantry was crucial to Lenin's whole view of the Russian revolution.

For the time being, 'steps toward socialism' was just a minor note in Lenin's rhetoric. The situation that greeted Lenin when he arrived in revolutionary Petrograd was still extremely fluid. Immediately after the abdication of the tsar on 2 March, two power centres had emerged in the nation's capital: the Petrograd Soviet, created from below by workers and soldiers inspired by memories of 1905, and the Provisional Government, created by members of the tsarist Duma in an effort to provide elite continuity. The Provisional Government may have looked solid and imposing, but even at the beginning of the revolution it was something of a phantom, with less real power and less legitimacy than the Petrograd Soviet. In fact the Provisional Government existed only at the sufferance of the Soviet, whose leadership did not want to take on the mantle of official government authority themselves. The Soviet therefore gave support to the Provisional Government *postolku-poskolku* – 'insofar as' – the Provisional Government carried out the policies of the Soviet.

Meanwhile the situation in the country was rapidly disintegrating under the pressure of a series of interlocking crises, of which the continuing war by Russia against Germany and Austria constituted the most inexorable. The Provisional Government supported the war effort due to traditional great-power concerns. The Soviet made all sorts of diplomatic efforts to achieve a democratic peace, but in the meantime it felt that Russia had to conduct 'revolutionary defence' – a defence not of tsarism, but of free Russia. But the country was simply incapable of conducting an unpopular and burdensome war, and a renewed military offensive in June ended in disaster.

The immediate trigger of the February revolution that overthrew the tsar was food-supply difficulties and the unbearably high cost of living, and the revolution only accelerated the spiralling economic breakdown. Tied to the crisis of the economy was the peasant demand for land. The Provisional Government insisted that such a fundamental question as land relations had to be settled by a Constitutional Assembly, but its insistence was caused less by democratic scruples than by fear of taking some very tough decisions with implications for the fundamental interests of the entire elite. No wonder that the eight-month history of the Provisional Government is one of desperate improvisation, as one hastily assembled coalition collapsed and gave way to the next. The only constant feature of these cabinets was the presence of Alexander Kerensky, a lawyer and Duma member with ties to the peasant parties. Kerensky more or less inserted himself into the very first cabinet as the representative of Soviet democracy, and gradually became almost the entire government himself. Faced with an impossible task, Kerensky made a valiant effort by means of charisma and bluster to keep Russia from imploding under the weight of its many contradictions. Coalition after coalition took over the reins of government and was promptly discredited by the ongoing war, by the accelerating economic and social collapse, by the postponement of agrarian reform.

The disenchantment of the masses with coalition government made the Bolshevik scenario seem like a plausible response to Russia's interlocking crises. Ultimately the success of Lenin and the Bolsheviks in 1917 was based on the success of the message they sent to the workers, soldiers and peasants. This message can be conveyed in three words and a punctuation mark: 'Take the power!' 'Power' here translates *vlast*, a word that could also be translated as 'sovereign authority', the ultimate source of legitimacy and decision-making. Everybody in Russia realized that the key question that confronted the country after the abdication of the tsar was the identity of the *vlast*. Everybody realized that only a *tverdaia vlast*, a strong and tough-minded sovereign authority, could effectively respond to the multiple crises buffeting Russian society.

The Bolsheviks insisted that 'the nature of the class that holds the *vlast* decides everything' – and they meant *everything*.[25] They told the Russian *narod* that as long as the *vlast* was controlled by their class enemies – the landowner, the capitalist, the 'bourgeois' in whatever form – the imperialist war would continue, the economic collapse would continue, the postponement of radical land reform would continue. Troubles would cease only when the workers as a class took the power and fulfilled their historical mission of leading the *narod* to revolutionary victory.

Lenin argued that a proletarian *vlast* was necessary for a strong and effective state. According to a common misunderstanding of Lenin's message in 1917, however, Lenin advanced the semi-anarchist slogan of 'smash the state!' This distortion of Lenin's message is taken from *State and Revolution*, Lenin's most famous book from 1917. This production is based on reading done in early 1917 before the outbreak of revolution in Russia and published in 1918 and it strikingly lacks the tang of Russia during the year of revolution. It is pitched at an abstract level of socialist revolution in general and consists mainly of angry polemics about the meaning of various passages from Marx and Engels. The phrase 'smash the state' is shorthand for the following slogan: 'Smash the bourgeois state and replace it with a strong and effective proletarian state.' The bourgeois state apparatus is smashed when (a) it cannot be used to repress the revolution and (b) it is thoroughly democratized. The proletarian state is *not* smashed – rather, it gradually dies out as society is transformed.

Lenin wanted to smash the bourgeois *state* apparatus, but he had a very different view of the bourgeois *economic* apparatus. This apparatus, perfected and given vast powers by the wartime state, must be carefully preserved and used as a ready-made tool by the revolutionary class. A perfect symbol for the imperialist economic apparatus was Germany's *Waffen- und Munitionsbeschaffungsamt* (Weapons and Ammunition Supply Department), or WUMBA for short. Lenin's vision of socialist revolution can be paraphrased as 'WUMBA for the people'. As he wrote in December 1916:

> The war has proved with special clarity and also in practical terms the truth that, before the war, was repeated by all the *vozhdi* of socialism that have now gone over to the bourgeoisie: contemporary capitalist society, especially in the advanced countries, has fully matured for the transition to socialism.
>
> If, for instance, Germany can direct the economic life of 66 million people *from a single centre*, and strain the energies of the *narod* to wage a predatory war in the interests of 100 or 200 financial magnates or aristocrats, the monarchy, etc., then the same can be done, in the interests of nine-tenths of the population, by the non-propertied masses, if their struggle is directed by the purposive workers, liberated from social-imperialist and social-pacifist influence . . . Expropriate the banks and, relying on the masses, carry out in their interests the *very same thing* WUMBA is carrying out in Germany![26]

Lenin's response to the crises of 1917 is best expressed, not by *State and Revolution*, but by two pamphlets from autumn 1917, one on the economic crisis (*The Threatening Catastrophe and How to Deal with It*) and the other on the political crisis (*Can the Bolsheviks Retain State Power?*).[27] Here Lenin sets out at length the programme I have summarized as 'Take the power!' and 'WUMBA for the people'. These slogans were intertwined. A key theme in Lenin's rhetoric is emblazoned in a chapter title from one of Lenin's pamphlets: 'Control Measures Are Known to All and Easy to Take'.[28] Land to the peasant, extensive economic regulation, peace diplomacy – these policies were all supported by the political rivals of the Bolsheviks, at least officially. And so, Lenin insisted, the *only* reason (and Lenin literally meant *only*) that these policies were not carried out was the inherent class nature of the bourgeois *vlast*.

Lenin's pamphlets from autumn 1917 also contain the famous and revealing image of the cook administering the state. The Russian word used by Lenin – *kukarkha*, a female cook – makes clear that he is alluding to the notorious circular of the tsarist education official cited in chapter One that discouraged the education of the children of cooks and similar persons:

> We are not utopians. We know that an unskilled workman or a *kukharka* is not capable of stepping immediately into the administration of the state. In this we agree with the [liberal] Kadets, with Breshkovskaya, and with Tsereteli [leading figures in the SR and Menshevik parties respectively]. But we are different from these citizens in that we demand an immediate break with the prejudice that that only the rich, or *chinovniki* [bureaucrats] from rich families, are in a position to *administer* the state, and to carry out the ordinary, day-to-day work of administration.[29]

Lenin is here truly Ilich, that is, son of Ilya, the educational reformer who fought within the tsarist system to make schools as widely available as possible.

Thus Lenin's heroic scenario gave the Bolsheviks a programme that struck many as a plausible response to the accelerating crisis – and struck others as unmitigated demagoguery. The resulting polarization first came to a head in July 1917, when a popular demonstration against the Provisional Government almost turned into an attempted *coup d'état*. Lenin did not support any attempt at a coup at this time because he felt that the project of a government based on the soviets did not yet have strong majority support. Nevertheless, the Bolshevik party was implicated and orders were

Lenin's hideout near Lake Razliv, Finland, August 1917.

issued for the arrest of Lenin, Zinoviev, Trotsky (who had now joined the Bolshevik party) and other leaders. Lenin and Zinoviev evaded arrest and holed up in a hut near Lake Razliv in Finland, not too far from Petrograd (Krupskaya remained in Petrograd). Lenin had once more returned to the underground.

The real turning point came in August 1917. The forces of order – the army, the landowners, the bureaucracy and the businessmen – did not fail to perceive the phantom status of the Provisional Government and began to pin their hopes on the new head of the army, Lavr Kornilov. Kornilov's confused attempt at a coup was beaten back by the combined efforts of the socialist parties, but the Bolsheviks were the ones who reaped the political credit.

Understandably so – the socialist moderates had wagered on a strategy of coalitions uniting socialists and non-socialists, a strategy widely perceived as bankrupt. The masses began to agree with the Bolsheviks: a coalition *vlast* was a bourgeois *vlast*, and the bourgeois *vlast* was leading the country to ruin.

The accelerating polarization of Russian society confirmed what can be termed the *ili-ili* (either-or) strategy of the Bolsheviks. As Stalin wrote in August 1917:

> Either, or!
> Either with the landlords and capitalists, and then the complete triumph of the counterrevolution.
> Or with the proletariat and the poor peasantry, and then the complete triumph of the revolution.
> The policy of conciliation and coalition is doomed to failure.[30]

The moderate socialists followed the contrasting logic of *ni-ni*: *neither* the counterrevolutionary forces of the right *nor* the extremist forces on the left – neither Kornilov nor Lenin – but rather a broad coalition of constructive forces. The concrete makeup of the various coalitions shifted over the year, but they were always based on *ni-ni* logic. But the moderate socialists who placed their political wager on *ni-ni* coalitions saw their original prestige dissolve and their reputations destroyed.

Starting in September, Lenin began to bombard his fellow Bolsheviks with letters, articles, whatever it took, in order to convince them that the time for an uprising had come and could not be delayed. The stars were now all in alignment: coalition-mongering was completely discredited, the Bolsheviks had substantial majorities in the most important soviets, the peasants were taking matters into their own hands, a revolutionary situation was brewing in other countries at war. Any delay would mean a disastrous acceleration of economic and military collapse.

At a small meeting of Bolshevik leaders on 10 October Lenin got his way on the main point: the course was set for a seizure of power. Lenin wanted an immediate armed uprising but his party comrades steered a more prudent course. The Second Congress of Soviets, a gathering of representatives from local soviets throughout the country, was due to meet in a couple of weeks, and the Bolsheviks could connect the insurrection to the opening of the Second Congress. The Petrograd Soviet – now with a Bolshevik majority and chaired by Lev Trotsky – organized a Military Revolutionary Committee. This committee, created openly and legally, became the organ of insurrection and on the night of 24 October it deposed the Provisional Government by force. The Second Congress then accepted the greatness thrust on them by the Bolsheviks and announced the formation of a new *vlast*, one based directly on the soviets. On 25 October, Lenin emerged from hiding to announce that 'the oppressed masses will themselves create a *vlast*', one in which 'the bourgeoisie will have no share whatsoever'.[31] The next day, he became Chairman of an all-Bolshevik Council of People's Commissars.

In the chaotic days that followed, the new Bolshevik state began to emerge. Lenin desired and expected a coalition with the Left Socialist Revolutionaries as the representative of the peasants in 'the revolutionary dictatorship of the workers and peasants'. Otherwise, he was dead set against anything that smelled of coalition or 'conciliation'. Through much shuffling and hard-nosed negotiation at the top Lenin got his way, mainly because the masses shared his disgust with coalition.

Although the Bolsheviks were committed to holding elections for a Constituent Assembly, they accorded no legitimacy to anything but a *vlast* based directly on the soviets. When the Constituent Assembly met in Petrograd on 5 January 1918 it was met with the demand that it recognize the sovereign authority of the soviets (and therefore the Bolshevik government). When the assembly refused, it was forcibly disbanded. The spirit of *ili-ili*, of polarization and civil war, had triumphed.

Petrograd to Moscow

On 12 March 1918 Lenin and Krupskaya again pulled up roots and boarded another train, this time accompanied by the entire Bolshevik government. For reasons of military security, Moscow was deemed a safer home for the new Soviet state than Petrograd. Lenin and Krupskaya were given rather spartan rooms in the Kremlin, adjoining the meeting rooms for the new government. This was the last move for Lenin. He never again left Moscow except to relax in nearby dachas (summer cottages).

Three train rides, three Lenins: in 1914 an obscure émigré seeking safe haven in wartime Europe, in 1917 a revolutionary politician emerging from the underground, in 1918 a grimly determined statesman travelling with the government of all the Russias.

The Bolshevik revolution in October 1917 had been a huge gamble, and even survival of the new 'proletarian *vlast*' was doubtful for most of the year 1918. Yet by the end of that year and for the first half of 1919 Lenin claimed that 'things have turned out just as we said they would'. For a brief period he was a truly happy man, convinced that his heroic scenario was rapidly coming true on a global scale.

Before arriving at this point, however, Lenin had to face what seemed like an endless succession of crises. In 3 March 1918 a humiliating peace treaty was signed with Germany at Brest-Litovsk. Lenin had to use all his influence to compel the reluctant Bolsheviks to sign. On 6 July the Left SRs staged their own uprising in protest against the foreign and domestic policies of their coalition partners. The crushing of the uprising by the Bolsheviks was accompanied

Lev Trotsky at Brest-Litovsk in 1918, where he led the delegation that negotiated the painful peace treaty with Germany.

by an end to meaningful electoral competition in local and central soviets. In the summer civil war and intervention intensified. On 30 August Lenin was shot and severely wounded by an SR terrorist. In response the Bolsheviks unleashed what they termed a Red Terror against the 'class enemy'.[32]

Out of this kaleidoscope of crises we shall take one Lenin document and try to see it in its full historical context. This particular document was only released after the fall of the Soviet Union and has since become rather notorious – indeed, it is often used as a sort of shorthand for the essential meaning of Lenin's career. It is a telegram sent on 11 August 1918 to Bolsheviks in Penza, a province about 700 kilometres southeast of Moscow in the Volga region. Lenin demands energetic repression of peasant revolts that he blamed on kulaks (rich peasants):

October 1918: Lenin shows the world he has recovered from his wounds by talking with his friend and secretary, Vladimir Bonch-Bruevich.

To Comrades Kuraev, Bosh, Minkin and other Penza communists:
Comrades! The uprising in five counties by the kulaks must lead to *merciless* suppression. This is demanded by the interest of the *whole* revolution, for there is now *everywhere* 'the last decisive battle' with kulakdom. An example needs to be set.

1. Hang (it must be hanging, so that the *narod sees*) *no fewer than one hundred* notorious kulaks, rich people, bloodsuckers.
2. Publish their names.
3. Extract *all* grain from them.
4. Designate hostages, in accordance with yesterday's telegram.

Do this in such a way that for hundreds of miles around the *narod* sees, thrills, knows, cries out: *they are strangling* and will strangle the bloodsucker kulaks.

Telegraph receipt and *implementation*.
Yours, Lenin
PS: Find people who are *tougher*.[33]

Why did Lenin insist that 'the interest of the revolution as a whole' demanded this grisly display of violence? His primary motivation was the food-supply crisis, that is, the need to feed people living in the cities, soldiers in the army and even those peasants who lived in the grain-deficit areas of Russia. From the outbreak of war in 1914 food-supply difficulties had been the motor that drove the unrelenting economic breakdown. Lack of exchange items, transportation problems and local embargoes had led to severe food shortages, and these in turn led to further economic, social and political dislocation. The Bolshevik's two predecessor governments – the tsarist and Provisional Government – had both moved steadily toward compulsory delivery of surpluses as a solution to the crisis. Surpluses (*izlishki*) were defined as all grain above a certain amount that was reserved for the peasant's own consumption and sowing.

All three regimes of the period – tsarist, Provisional Government and Bolshevik – strove to use material incentives to obtain grain, but all three were willing to use force to ensure delivery by grain producers. The tsarist and Provisional Government each collapsed, in large part due to their ineffective food-supply policies, and their collapse only further intensified the direness of Russia's situation. The Bolsheviks had to come up with an effective response or they too would join their predecessors in the dustbin of history.

The sharpness of the crisis was intensified in summer 1918 by the consequences of the Brest-Litovsk treaty and the incipient civil war. Crucial grain-surplus regions – Ukraine, Volga, Siberia, North Caucasus – were cut off by German occupation and hostilities in the Volga region. Under these circumstances any grain-surplus region that remained under Bolshevik control became crucial, and so the Bolsheviks pinned their survival hopes on provinces like Penza. In August 1918 Lenin dashed off many telegrams on food-supply policy that show him desperately trying to get grain by any means. Providing bonuses for prompt delivery was the central strategy: 'Give out bonuses to counties and villages in the form of equipment, money for schools and hospitals and, in general, predominantly for such aims.' Lenin urged helping with the harvest, plus extensive agitation efforts to explain why the grain was needed. He hoped to get grain from former landowner estates that were now state farms run by poor peasants. He also demanded the taking of hostages 'from among the rich' and other applications of force to ensure compulsory deliveries. To cite only Lenin's telegrams that mandate the use of bonuses as material incentives would of course be seriously misleading. To cite only his telegrams demanding the use of force is equally misleading.[34]

The repression that Lenin demanded in the telegram to Penza was occasioned by a peasant uprising in protest against compulsory food-supply deliveries that broke out on 5 August 1918. Peasants in the village of Kuchi killed five Red Army soldiers and three members of the local soviet. The rebellion spread to other villages close by. All this was happening 45 kilometres from the civil-war front, which partly explains Lenin's panicky response. Despite Lenin's demands for a hundred hangings, the rebellion was quelled by August 12 by shooting thirteen ringleaders in the village of Kuchi for being directly responsible for the deaths of state representatives.

Do we need to resort to Lenin's individual personality or to his ideological scenario in order to explain his demand in the Penza telegram for grisly reprisals against violent rebellion? Neither explanation seems likely, as shown by similar actions taken by people who did not share Lenin's personality or his ideology, but who did share his objective problem, namely, establishing a new political authority in conditions of social chaos and economic breakdown. One non-Bolshevik activist, A. V. Peshekhonov, later recalled waking up one morning in Rostov under one of the anti-Bolshevik White governments and finding corpses hanging from the lampposts all over town, by order of the government.[35]

Nevertheless, knowledge of Lenin's heroic scenario is needed to make full sense of the Penza telegram. Lenin insists that the *narod* should *see* the hangings. Why? to terrorize them? Not in Lenin's mind. Lenin was convinced that the *narod* hated the 'bloodsucker kulaks' and would praise the worker *vlast* for taking them on. The executions were meant as a form of inspiring class leadership. As such, they played a part in a narrative that Lenin was telling himself and others in autumn 1918. According to Lenin, civil-war battles had provoked kulak uprisings such as the one in Penza and these in turn accelerated the workings of his heroic scenario. Lenin's long-held scenario outlined, first, a political revolution against the tsar in alliance with the *whole* peasantry and, second, a socialist revolution made possible by the urban proletariat's growing influence over the rural proletariat and semi-proletariat. The revolution of October 1917 had been in alliance with the *whole* peasantry and thus, by the logic of Lenin's own scenario, it was essentially a political rather than a true socialist revolution. Lenin's loyalty to his scenario is shown by his eagerness in late 1918 to announce that kulak rebellions had kick-started a new phase of the revolution, one in which the kulak exploiters were finally sloughed off from the revolutionary coalition, thus allowing the workers to fight alongside *only* the exploited labourers in the village.

Lenin seems to be actually encouraged by this loss of a class ally. The heart of Marxism is the claim that only those who themselves are exploited can build socialism. The Russian revolution could therefore truly be called a socialist one only when the workers were allied with the exploited labourers in the countryside, and with no one else. Thus Lenin insisted in late 1918 that the class conflict taking place during in the most remote villages of Russia portended a revolution whose significance was 'incomparably deeper and greater' than the Bolshevik October revolution of 1917:

> This [new phase of] struggle has cut off the property-owning and exploiting classes from the revolution completely; it definitely puts our revolution on the socialist road, just as the urban working class had tried so hard and vigorously to do in October [1917]. The working class will not be able to direct the revolution successfully along this road unless it finds firm, deliberate and solid support in the countryside.[36]

In his polemic against Kautsky written in autumn 1918 during his convalescence from the attempt on his life – *Renegade Kautsky and the Proletarian Revolution* – Lenin argued that the proletariat's proven ability to 'rally the village poor around itself against the rich peasants' was a sign that Russia was in fact ripe for socialist revolution, contrary to Kautsky's claim. The pre-war Kautsky – 'Kautsky when he was a Marxist' – understood this. Why did the renegade Kautsky of 1918 deny it, just when 'things have turned out just as we said they would'?[37] This reasoning convinced Lenin that food-supply difficulties were sparking 'the last, final struggle' with kulakdom (to use the apocalyptic words of the Internationale, the socialist hymn quoted in the Penza telegram). In reality, these same difficulties were prodding food-supply officials to make a much more pragmatic response. The attempt to use 'class war in the villages' to obtain grain had clearly backfired, causing a definite retreat toward new food-supply policies that aimed at meeting the peasant halfway. Lenin's rhetoric fully caught up with these shifts only in 1919.

The second October that Lenin believed he saw going on in the countryside was not the only good news he received in late 1918. He ended his book-length polemic against 'renegade Kautsky' by writing:

Lenin at his desk in the Kremlin in late 1918, after recovering from his wounds.

The above lines were written on 9 November 1918. That same night news was received from Germany announcing the beginning of a victorious revolution, first in Kiel and other northern towns and ports, where the *vlast* has passed into the hands of Soviets of worker and soldier deputies, then in Berlin, where, too, the *vlast* has passed into the hands of the Soviet.

The conclusion that still remained to be written to my pamphlet on Kautsky and on the proletarian revolution is now superfluous.[38]

The Bolsheviks were confident that a revolutionary chain-reaction starting in Germany was now unstoppable, a conviction hardly dented by the crushing of the radical socialist Spartacist rebellion in January 1919 and the murder of its leaders Rosa Luxemburg and Karl Liebknecht. In March 1919 a hastily convened and not very representative meeting was held in Moscow to found the long-awaited Third International, which would consist solely

Headlines in the Canadian newspaper *The Globe,* January 1919.

of parties purified of any taint of opportunism. Lenin exultantly claimed that the world revolution was now moving forward with 'the torrential might of millions and tens of millions of workers sweeping everything from their path'.[39]

Krupskaya tells us that the news of the German revolution made the first anniversary of the revolution 'some of the happiest days of Lenin's life'. The British journalist Arthur Ransome, interviewing Lenin in early 1919, felt that 'more than ever, Lenin struck me as a happy man . . . His whole faith is in the elemental forces that move people, his faith in himself is merely his belief that he justly estimates the direction of these forces.'[40] In this mood of happy confidence, Lenin once again alluded to the frustrated dreams of his brother:

> Comrades, behind us there is a long line of revolutionaries who sacrificed their lives for the emancipation of Russia. The lot of the majority of these revolutionaries was a hard one. They suffered

150

March 1919: Lenin chairs the first congress of the new Third International in Moscow.

the persecution of the tsarist government, but it was not their good fortune to see the triumph of the revolution. The happiness that has fallen to our lot is all the greater. Not only have we seen the triumph of our revolution, not only have we seen it become consolidated amidst unprecedented difficulties, creating a new kind of *vlast* and winning the sympathy of the whole world, but we are also seeing the seed sown by the Russian revolution springing up in Europe.[41]

Lenin's mood of optimism came only after a year of life-and-death crises. What we may call his 'anniversary period' started in autumn 1918 around the time of the first anniversary of the October revolution and lasted until summer 1919. In Lenin's confident view during this period the Russian workers were leading the country down the road toward socialism. Despite all the difficulties and challenges, further progress down that road was guaranteed – at home by the class war in the villages, and abroad by the incipient

7 November 1918: Lenin marks the first anniversary of the 1917 revolution by giving a speech at the unveiling of a monument to Marx and Engels in Revolution Square, Moscow: 'We are living through a happy time . . .'.

socialist revolution. The heroic scenario of the proletariat as the *vozhd* of the *narod* was vindicated. As Lenin put it on 7 November 1918 at the unveiling of a monument in Moscow to Marx and Engels:

The great world-historic service of Marx and Engels is that they showed the workers of the world their role, their task, their mission, namely, to be the first to rise in the revolutionary struggle against capital and to unite around themselves in this struggle *all* working and exploited people.

We are living through a happy time, when this prophecy of the great socialists is beginning to be realized.[42]

5

Beyond the 'Textbook à la Kautsky'

In early 1923, weeks before his final incapacitating stroke, Lenin wrote about Karl Kautsky for the last time: 'It need hardly be said that a textbook written à la Kautsky [*po kautskomu*] was a very useful thing in its day. But it is time, for all that, to abandon the idea that it foresaw all the forms of development of subsequent world history. It would be timely to say that those who think so are simply fools.'[1]

The contrast between this dour assertion and Lenin's mood during what I have termed his 'anniversary period' – late 1918 through summer 1919 – is striking. During the anniversary period Lenin called Kautsky a renegade because Kautsky was turning his back on his own earlier predictions just as they were coming true. But looking back in 1923 Lenin stated in effect that only a fool would claim (as he himself had done in 1918) that 'things have turned out just as we said they would'.

Lenin's heroic scenario had always been very strongly rooted in the 'textbook à la Kautsky' – orthodox 'revolutionary Social Democracy' of the Second International – and he had gloried in the fact. When and why did he move from his usual stance of aggressive unoriginality to one of reluctant originality? According to the most common account, Lenin's rethinking began in early 1921 with the introduction of the New Economic Policy (NEP). Up to late 1920 (we are told) Lenin and the Bolsheviks were so carried away with a feeling of euphoria that they started to believe that harsh civil-war policies – later given the name of 'war communism' – represented a short cut or even a leap into full communism. Only economic collapse and peasant rebellion in the winter of 1920–21 convinced them of their mistake. Lenin finally began to understand that the peasants required material incentives in order to produce. The process of rethinking culminated in the bundle of articles and drafts from late 1922 and early 1923 that were later termed 'Lenin's testament'. Some writers view Lenin's rethinking as fundamental, others as relatively superficial, but all tie it strongly to NEP.

The standard account is profoundly misleading. In reality Lenin's rethinking began in 1919, just as soon as he realized that things were *not* 'turning out just as we said they were'. There was no mass euphoria among the Bolsheviks in 1920, no collective hallucination that Russia was on the eve of full communism. On the contrary the Bolsheviks were painfully aware of the manifold compromises and defeats that were leading them *away* from socialism. The dramatic changes that came with the introduction of NEP in 1921 were just another round of painful compromises. Lenin's outlook in his final writings can be traced back to concerns that began to surface in 1919.

In what follows we focus on Lenin's personal evolution. Lenin had been very explicit about the Marxist justification for undertaking a socialist revolution in backward Russia. Abroad, the Russian revolution would spark off revolutions in more advanced countries. At home, the workers had moved beyond the alliance with the peasantry as a whole. Since they were now allied solely with the exploited labourers in the villages, they were free to move on from a merely democratic revolution to the socialist revolution. Lenin was equally insistent that 'soviet democracy' had the mission of utterly remaking the state apparatus by cleansing it of 'bureaucratism'. He was therefore profoundly disappointed when he was forced to realize that these things were not happening – not in the short term, nor even in the medium term. Like a cartoon character who keeps walking in midair even though he has left the cliff behind, Lenin no longer had the solid basis of his original scenario to support his journey. He had to come up with an explanation of why Russia's socialist revolution was not doomed to crash to the ground.

All through his life Lenin had always stressed the continuity of his views. He argued that the 1905 revolution vindicated the pre-revolutionary *Iskra* platform, that his wartime Left Zimmerwald platform did not deviate from Kautsky-when-he-was-a-Marxist, and that the October revolution had orthodox Marxist credentials. From 1919 he was forced to admit that some basic Bolshevik assumptions had not yet been vindicated, yet true to his life-long habit he minimized the extent of the necessary modifications. In the 1923 article quoted above, he characterized his changes to the 'textbook à la Kautsky' as 'certain amendments (quite insignificant from the standpoint of the general development of world history) . . . certain distinguishing features . . . certain partial innovations . . . somewhat unusual conditions . . . such details of development (from the standpoint of world history they were certainly details) as the Brest-Litovsk peace, the New Economic Policy, and so forth'.[2]

To understand the adjustments that Lenin was forced to make to his heroic scenario, we need to take a look at some of these 'details of development' that may have been small in the scale of world history but that loomed large in the scale of the few years remaining to Lenin.

The Challenge of Events

From many points of view Bolshevik survival was a miracle and Lenin felt that, no matter what else was urged against Bolshevism, the survival of the proletarian *vlast* was a bottom-line justification for the great deed of October 1917. Yet he could not hide from himself that some fundamental expectations had not been met.

Between 1918 and 1922 there were so many challenges to Bolshevik rule that it is perhaps better to speak of 'civil wars' in the plural. The Whites, who relied principally on the elite classes of tsarist Russia, were led by former officers such as Admiral Kolchak in Siberia and General Denikin in south Russia. Peasant rebels, collectively called the Greens, mounted a series of revolts both local and large-scale. National minorities in the border regions also took advantage of the temporary breakdown of central authority to declare independence. Some were successful (Poland, Finland, Baltic states); others were reincorporated into Soviet Russia. Finally, foreign powers such as France, the United States and Japan intervened in the hope of toppling Bolshevism.

Given the many challenges to its existence, the most crucial accomplishment of the new government was the creation of the Red Army out of the ruins of the old Imperial army. The Red Army was a most improbable institution. The Bolsheviks – a radical working-class party that strongly opposed militarism and preached defeatism before the revolution – not only had to turn themselves into military commanders but also had to work together with tsarist military officers and peasant recruits in order to build an effective fighting machine.

In the vivid phrase of eyewitness Arthur Ransome, the Bolsheviks had 'illusion after illusion scraped from them by the pumice-stone of experience'.[3] Informed outsiders, each writing before the introduction of NEP in 1921, detailed the failure of Lenin's three basic justifications during this period. The American socialist Morris Hillquit detailed the disappointing record of international revolution:

Only when the Sparticide risings in Germany were quelled [in early 1919] and the Hungarian Soviet government was overthrown [in mid-1919]; when the great struggle in the Italian metal industry was settled by mutual concessions, and the oft-announced general strikes in England systematically failed to materialize; when the spirit of unrest and rebellion engendered by the war and the Versailles 'settlement' was succeeded by a state of sullen apathy, and the capitalist world settled down to a spell of heavy political reaction, only then did the Communists begin to lose faith in an imminent world revolution.[4]

Socialist transformation in the countryside also came up short. As émigré Russian economist Leo Pasvolsky drily observed about hopes for a significant movement toward collective agricultural production, the Bolsheviks 'made attempts to produce new agrarian forms, but they did not expect any great success out of them and did not achieve any success'.[5] Pasvolsky was no doubt correct about the expectations of the Bolsheviks in general, but Lenin himself had started off with more sanguine hopes about what could be accomplished during and even because of the wartime economic emergency.

William Walling (the American socialist whose interview with Lenin after the 1905 revolution was quoted in chapter Three) was equally dismissive about Bolshevik attempts to remake the state apparatus when he derided 'the inability of a party consisting almost wholly of agitators, propagandists and self-appointed shepherds of the proletariat to furnish any administrative, technical or constructive talents'.[6]

All three of these contemporaneous observers were hostile to Bolshevism. Yet, as we shall see, Lenin did not deny these disappointments and indeed, in certain moods, could be even more scathing about them.

In early 1921, when the Bolsheviks introduced the New Economic Policy or NEP, the Soviet government carried out a series of dramatic reversals of economic policy. Private trade in grain was legalized or, perhaps better, decriminalized, while state industry was forced to work for the market and to adopt 'capitalist' methods. These

The rebellion of what used to be the enthusiastically loyal garrison at Kronstadt helped concentrate the minds of the Bolshevik leadership on the need to introduce the New Economic Policy in early 1921. Taken on 22 March 1921, this photograph shows Lenin and Trotsky (standing front centre) with delegates of the Tenth Party Congress who participated in crushing the rebellion.

changes roughly coincided with the end of hostilities, the signing of peace and trade treaties and the consequent demobilization of the Red Army. The dramatic introduction of NEP has also created a tendency to see the year 1921 as the end of the Russian's prolonged time of troubles. But in many respects the real year of transition was 1922, a time when Russia finally emerged from the long years of collapse and breakdown and the Bolshevik party stopped reeling from the rapid changes resulting from the introduction and then the unplanned extension of NEP in 1921. A closer look at 1922 will give us a better idea of the context of Lenin's final evolution.

After years of economic degradation a drought in 1921 set off an intense famine that provided the climax to the horror and devastation of the civil war. Russia could hardly have coped with this famine without the benign intervention of foreign aid, particularly by the American Relief Agency (ARA). At the beginning of 1922 the country was still completely in the grip of this famine. By the end of the year the worst was over and the country was beginning to revive. The change can be traced in a small book appropriately entitled *Plague, Pestilence and Famine*. It consists of letters from a British nurse, Muriel Payne, who spent March–September 1922 in the famine region along the Volga. At the beginning of the book, Payne is confronted with something out of Dante's *Inferno*:

> The chaos of the whole country is indescribable. No one seems to know anything, or to do anything. The population is a seething mass of louse-covered, ragged humanity, who, apparently, have no purpose left in life. They all move slowly and listlessly about, the reigning law being, 'It is yours, take it'. But there is no nothing left to take, so they just sit down and die.[7]

One story will give the flavour of the heartbreaking realities:

> We came across a barn full of dead people. They were not just heaped up, but were carefully arranged like waxwork figures – some standing, some sitting, and some had tumbled down as the thaw had set in. In the hand of each was a piece of paper with the name of the person and a recommendation from the priest to St Peter to allow them through when he had time to attend to it.[8]

During the time of Payne's stay, the country began to crawl out of the abyss, as shown by the contrast in Moscow's appearance at the beginning and end of her time in Russia:

> Moscow, March 1922: 'Everything is indescribably miserable and sordid. Streets look as though they have never been streets. Houses are falling to bits – ruins of the Revolution. There is a

continuous stream of ragged, silent men and women, an occasional horse and sleigh, or a motor car flying the red flag. . . . There are no shops worth mentioning.'[9]

Moscow, September 1922: 'Moscow is a different place since I was here six months ago. Shops are open and apparently flourishing, there is plenty of food (at exorbitant prices) for those who can afford to buy. Trams are running, opera playing, and people are much better dressed. You can get quite a fair dinner for 20 million roubles!'[10]

Payne rather enjoyed herself at a parade for 'young Communists' and even managed to join the procession. She reports that 'Lloyd George was burnt in the evening, for what particular sin I don't know'.

It was altogether a strange sight; but rather fine to see the men, women and children in rags marching side by side with better dressed people. There was something striking, too, about the simplicity of it all – the 'Grand Stand' (a small wooden platform holding all the Bolsheviks packed together like sardines), so crowded and uncomfortable, with only a chair for the speaker to stand on to raise him above the shoulders of the rest.[11]

Payne's attitude toward the Bolsheviks is mixed. She is bemused that a starving country is still obsessed with preventing one peasant from hiring another. She observes that 'the power of Moscow does not extend very far in practice – 200 miles perhaps beyond the city'. Nevertheless, she is impressed that 'whatever the reason, after travelling more than two thousand miles across Russia, one cannot help being struck with the comparative law and order exhibited by this population of millions under the rule of party of less than 500,000 men'. She finally divided the party into two: the idealists

May Day 1920: to Lenin's left is his old comrade Lev Kamenev.

who 'not only dream of a glorious and happy Russia, but who work for her good with no pay, no thanks, no holidays, no health; who still hope, and, I believe, still pray, and realize to the depths of their being the sorrows of the people' vs. the 'violent men, nominally their colleagues'.[12]

Lenin's Health

After Lenin's train trip from Petrograd to Moscow his life of peregrinations was over. The dramatic changes in his personal situation no longer came from enforced moves from place to place but rather from his deteriorating health. The final evolution in his outlook must be seen against the background of his growing awareness that his days were numbered.

The wear and tear of life begins to tell on Lenin, seen here at the funeral of his brother-in-law Mark Elizarov in March 1919.

All his working life Lenin was prone to overwork and to over-involvement with tense political issues, leading to nerves, headaches and insomnia.[13] Fortunately, he had always been able to regain his spiritual equilibrium by means of vacations, energetic walks in the mountains and a quiet family life. After becoming head of state in 1917 these safety valves were no longer available in the same way. Looking back, he ironically thanked his political enemies, since their accusation of his being a German spy in 1917 forced him into hiding and thus gave him his last real vacation.

Indications of the brain troubles that eventually finished him off were already cutting into Lenin's working habits by late 1920. By August 1921 he wrote to Maxim Gorky that 'I am so tired that I can't do a damned thing'.[14] Headaches, insomnia and inability to concentrate continued to make serious inroads into Lenin's workaholic ways. In December 1921 a week's vacation at his dacha residence in Gorki stretched out longer and longer, until finally the Politburo insisted that he take a vacation for six weeks. Lenin was able to return to work and to participate in the 11th Party Congress in March 1922, although he was very upset by his reduced ability to read documents and to meet with congress delegates. He later referred to his fainting spells during this period as 'the first bell' (at the third bell, the train leaves).

Whether the underlying problem was his health or the political contradictions of NEP Russia, 1922 was marked by particularly irritable and aggressive outbursts on Lenin's part that seemed to be aimed at permanently silencing independent views. The most egregious of these attempts were threats of violence against the Orthodox Church and the exile of many prominent socialist and non-socialist intellectuals.[15]

Lenin's doctors still had very little sense of the seriousness of his illness, and only after his first stroke on 27 May 1922 were its full dimensions glimpsed. This stroke temporarily took away his ability to speak clearly or write legibly. Lenin was profoundly pessimistic after his first stroke and assumed that the end had come. He was essentially correct about this, although temporary improvements gave him a few more months of work. He remembered that a peasant had once predicted that his life would end by means of a *kondrashka* (an old word for stroke). The peasant based his diagnosis on the fact that Lenin's neck was 'awfully short'.

Lenin also felt, based on his own observations, that professional revolutionaries tended to burn out by around the age of fifty. He recalled the double suicide of Paul and Laura Lafargue in 1911. With this example in front of him, Lenin now contemplated suicide. On 30 May 1922 he demanded to see Stalin at his dacha in Gorki. Stalin and Bukharin drove out, and Stalin saw Lenin alone for just a few minutes. While he was waiting, Bukharin remarked to Lenin's sister

Maria that he guessed the reason why Ilich wanted to see Stalin. Stalin came out of Lenin's room visibly shaken. While walking to the car, he conferred with Bukharin and Maria (while requesting that Krupskaya not be told). Lenin had reminded Stalin of a previous promise to help him in the case of paralysis, and he now wanted to call in his promise. He asked Stalin to obtain cyanide pills.

As the three talked near the car, Stalin was seized with doubts: 'I promised to do it in order to calm him, but what if he interprets my words as meaning that things really are hopeless?' So it was decided that Stalin would return and reassure Lenin that the doctors were optimistic, that Lenin would recover, and that the time to fulfil his request had not yet arrived. Lenin agreed, although as Stalin left Lenin said to him, 'are you playing games with me? [*Lukavil?*]'. Stalin answered, 'when have you ever seen me play games with you?'[16]

And in fact Lenin did improve, though several months passed before he was even allowed visitors. In August and September he was receiving political visits at Gorki and preparing for a return to work, which he did on 2 October. For the rest of the autumn months Lenin worked at a fairly intense pace. During this period he had disagreements with various Politburo members, including Stalin and Trotsky, but these disagreements were settled without disrupting the usual working relationships.

In late November Lenin evidently sensed that the end was rapidly approaching and that the time had come to bequeath a final statement to the party. He therefore asked to be sent a copy of the 'Political Testament' of Friedrich Engels.[17] On 15 December 1922 Lenin had his second stroke. He could no longer write legibly and could only communicate orally or by means of dictation (a procedure he strongly disliked). On the eve of this stroke he had already begun to 'liquidate' his various ongoing files and to dispose of the books in his personal library. Books on agriculture went to his sister Maria, books on education, scientific organization of labour and production propaganda went to Krupskaya, belles-lettres were

Lenin relaxing at Gorki, summer 1922.

to be held until needed, while he reserved for himself political writings, memoirs and biographies.[18] Cut off from current affairs, restricted to a few minutes of dictation a day, Lenin could influence affairs only by writing a few final articles.

Lenin's writings in the period December 1922 to March 1923 consist not only of articles published at the time but of various secret dictations that only came to light later. The precise intention of these secret writings is very difficult to assess and has given rise to long-standing controversies. Unfortunately, these controversies have deflected attention from the content of the articles that we know Lenin wanted to be published. These final articles contain Lenin's last thoughts on the three vulnerable points of his heroic scenario – international revolution, peasant support for socialist transformation, and remaking the state apparatus – and as such they arise organically out of the shift in outlook that began in 1919. In order to bring this out I will pass over the issue of Lenin's secret writings and examine his reaction to the three challenges, starting in 1919 and continuing on to early 1923.

Holding Out

Lenin's happy confidence in early 1919 about international revolution comes out in an interview conducted by the sympathetic Arthur Ransome. Ransome reported that Lenin 'was entirely convinced that England was on the eve of revolution, and pooh-poohed my objections . . . "Strikes and Soviets. If these two habits once get hold, nothing will keep the workmen from them. And Soviets, once started, must sooner or later come to supreme power".'[19] When Ransome stated that he did not believe there would be a revolution in Britain, Lenin responded:

> We have a saying that a man may have typhoid while still on his legs. Twenty, maybe thirty years ago I had abortive typhoid, and was going about with it, had had it some days before it knocked me over. Well, England and France and Italy have caught the disease already. England may seem to you to be untouched, but the microbe is already there.[20]

A year later, Lenin had talk with another visiting Englishman, Bertrand Russell, and was distinctly less sanguine. He outlined to Russell the strategy he wanted British Communists to adopt: support the election of a Labour government in the hopes that its inaction would radicalize the masses – a strategy obviously extrapolated from his own experience in 1917. When Russell opined that 'whatever is possible in England can be achieved without bloodshed, [Lenin] waved aside the suggestion as fantastic'. Nevertheless,

Lenin speaks at the Second Congress of the Communist International, July 1920. Seated to Lenin's left is Karl Radek.

Lenin 'admitted that there is little chance of revolution in England now, and that the working man is not yet disgusted with Parliamentary Government'.[21]

The delay in international revolution forced Lenin to be more cautious in his predictions of 'steps toward socialism' at home. In early 1919, despite the huge challenges that threatened the survival of the Bolshevik government, Lenin could still assure his audiences that 'this is the last difficult half-year' because 'the international situation has never been so good'.[22] He was particularly cheered by the revolution that broke out in Hungary in March 1919. As a 'more cultured country' than Russia, Hungary would show the socialist revolution in a better light, 'without the violence, without the bloodshed that was forced upon us by the Kerenskys and the imperialists'.[23]

Lenin's optimism could not be sustained. The defeat of the Hungarian revolution in August 1919 marks a turning-point in his rhetoric about international revolution. By early 1921, on the eve of NEP, he dolefully noted that the West European workers had failed to take advantage of the opportunity to 'have done with the capitalists at one stroke'. As a result, 'our main difficulties over the past four years have been due to the fact that the West European capitalists managed to bring the war to an end and stave off revolution'.[24] Lenin accordingly adjusted his scenario in a number of ways. One method was to lower the definition of success. Yes, the Bolsheviks may have been over-sanguine about receiving 'swift and direct support' from the European proletariat, but they had managed to survive and this meant that they had been 'correct on the most fundamental issues':

Lenin consults with Nikolai Bukharin (centre) and Grigory Zinoviev during sessions of the Second Congress of the Comintern, summer 1920.

When we ask ourselves how this could have happened, how it could be that a state, undoubtedly one of the most backward and weakest, managed to repel the attacks of the openly hostile, most powerful countries in the world, when we try to examine this question, we see clearly that it was because we proved to be correct on the most fundamental issues. Our forecasts and calculations proved to be correct. It turned out that although we did not receive the swift and direct support of the working people of the world that we had counted on, and which we had regarded as the basis of the whole of our policy, we did receive support of another kind, which was not direct or swift, namely, the sympathy of the labouring masses – the workers and the peasants, the masses in the countryside – throughout the world, even in those states that are most hostile to us.[25]

Despite the absence of actual revolution Lenin insisted that the Soviet system remained an inspirational model to the exploited people of the world. He even boasted that Soviet Russia was winning support from capitalists – specifically, the capitalists of the small countries bordering Russia who signed trade treaties with the Bolsheviks despite pressure from the victorious great powers.[26]

However, Lenin did not waver in his conviction that actual international revolution was a necessary basis for rapid steps toward socialism in Russia itself. In one of his final articles of 1923 Lenin took heart that 'Russia, India, China, etc.' made up the vast majority of mankind and 'this majority has been drawn into the struggle for liberation with extraordinary rapidity, so that in this respect there cannot be the slightest doubt what the final outcome of the world struggle will be. In this sense, the complete victory of socialism is fully and absolutely assured.' All socialist Russia had to do was hold out (*proderzhat'sia*) until the final victory. In this article of five printed pages Lenin not only uses 'hold out' twice, but also employs words with related meanings and based on the same root (*derzhat'*) for a total of six more times.[27]

Lenin's 'hold-out scenario' displays something of his old confidence, although in a more subdued tone. Yet the enforced dependence on international capitalism injected a new anxiety into his outlook. Old Bolshevism had fought for political freedom in Russia as a central goal because the Bolsheviks had been confident that the Social Democratic message could win the loyalty of the workers in an open fight. But now the fear of international capitalism made political freedom in Soviet Russia seem equivalent to suicide. As he wrote in 1921 to a party comrade who advocated full freedom of speech:

> Freedom of the press in the RSFSR [Russian Soviet Federated Socialist Republic], surrounded by bourgeois enemies of the entire world, means providing freedom *of political organization* to the bourgeoisie and their most loyal servants, the Mensheviks and the SRs.
>
> This is an incontrovertible fact.
>
> The bourgeoisie (on a global scale) are still stronger than us by many orders of magnitude. To give it *another* such weapon as freedom of political organization (= freedom of the press, for the press is the core and basis of political organization) means making the enemy's job easier and helping the class enemy.
>
> We do not wish to do away with ourselves by suicide and therefore we will not do this.[28]

Lenin's remarks show his old respect for 'freedom of the press' as the essence of 'freedom of political organization', but combined now with a new sense of vulnerability.

Kto-Kovo (Who-Whom)

Lenin's second justification for 'steps toward socialism' in Russia was the class war *within* the peasantry. From his very first writings in 1894 Lenin had seen the peasantry splitting apart into two poles, a majority of exploited proto-proletarians at one pole and a minority of exploiter proto-bourgeois at the other. The democratic revolution against the tsar would be fought alongside the *entire* peasantry, since the tsar's oppressive rule violated the interests of rich and poor peasant alike. The political freedom made possible by the tsar's overthrow would give the socialists access to the exploited rural majority. Support for a socialist revolution against capitalism would be forthcoming only from the exploited majority, not from the 'petty bourgeoisie'.

Lenin was still operating with this scenario when he announced in late 1918 that class conflict in the Russian village was leading to a rural October that was even more significant than the 1917 October revolution carried out by the urban workers. The socialist credentials of the Bolshevik revolution were vulnerable as long as the Bolsheviks were supported by the whole peasantry and not just the exploited majority.

Alas, the mismatch between scenario and reality could not long be ignored and Lenin was again forced to adjust. Before 1919 Lenin focused on the polar extremes within the peasantry: the rural poor (*bednota*) versus the kulak. In 1919 the official focus moved toward the *centre* of the spectrum: the mass of the peasantry that had not yet been polarized. More and more, steps toward socialism depended on enticing the middle peasant – the peasant as peasant – to follow the lead of the proletariat. Accordingly, Lenin's adjustments can be followed in a series of parallel processes: disillusion with the leadership qualities of the rural poor, soft-pedalling the conflict with the kulak and searching for ways to convince the middle peasant of the virtues of socialism.

Lenin addresses a conference of socialist communes in December 1918, when he is still relatively sanguine about the prospects of communes and state farms.

In Lenin's original scenario the rural poor were assigned a specific mission: to spearhead the transition from small-scale individual production to large-scale collective production. Impelled by the economic breakdown caused by the war, the poorest peasants would realize the impossibility of farming in the old ways. They would pool together their land to form communes (*kommuny*) or take over landowner estates and run them as 'state farms' (*sovkhozy*). These collective enterprises would reveal the advantages of socialism to the rest of the peasantry, and voilà! slow but steady and perceptible progress down the path to socialist transformation of the countryside. Such was Lenin's vision.

The only problem – as Lenin realized with growing dismay – was that the actual communes and state farms were *negative* examples that pushed the peasantry *away* from socialism. From early 1919 on we have a ceaseless litany of complaints that only increase in volume and bitterness. Lenin's vitriol on this issue stemmed from his enormous emotional investment in his original scenario.

> *April 1919*: 'The peasants say: long live the Soviet *vlast*, long live the Bolsheviks, but down with *kommuniia*! They curse the *kommuniia* when it is organized in a stupid way and forced upon them. They are suspicious of everything that is imposed upon them, and quite rightly so. We must go to the middle peasants, we must help them, teach them, but only in the field of science and socialism. In the area of farm management we must learn from them.'[29]

> *December 1919:* 'the communes have only succeeded in provoking a negative attitude among the peasantry, and the word "commune" has even at times become a slogan in the fight against communism'.[30]

> *December 1920:* Lenin states derisively that collectively organized farms were in such pathetic condition that they were justifiably termed almshouses.[31]

> *March 1921*: 'The experience of this collective farming shows us only an example of how *not* to farm: the surrounding peasants laugh or are filled with indignation.'[32]

Parallel to Lenin's progressive disillusionment with the rural poor as class leaders is a definite soft-pedalling of the frenetic anti-kulak rhetoric of 1918. In 1919 he emphasized the distinction between the kulak and the bourgeoisie in general: kulak resistance would be crushed but kulaks would not be expropriated like urban capitalists.[33] Later in the year he noted with some wonderment that the pitiless logic of '*ili-ili*' – *either* the dictatorship of the workers *or* the dictatorship of the landowners – meant that kulaks in Siberia supported soviet power against Admiral Kolchak (the 'supreme leader' of the anti-Bolshevik White movement). In December 1920 an irritated Lenin told Bolshevik questioners that the Central

Committee had unanimously agreed that 'we got carried away with the struggle against the kulak and lost all sense of measure'. By this time, in fact, the Bolsheviks were openly relying on the economic exertions of the kulak, although he had been rechristened for this purpose as 'the industrious owner'.[34]

As we see, Lenin had abandoned his original 'class war in the villages' scenario long before the introduction of NEP in early 1921. In its place arose a scenario whose protagonist was the previous walk-on role of the middle peasant. An official 'shift to the middle peasant' was inaugurated with much fanfare in early 1919. According to émigré economist Leo Pasvolsky, the open letters to the peasants written by Lenin and Trotsky, the various official decrees, and 'the dozens of articles that were devoted to the subject in the whole Soviet press for weeks after that . . . constitute the most elaborate scheme of agitation ever used for any one purpose by the Soviet regime'.[35] The peasants were quick to grasp that the soviet power was seeking a new base of social support and that the *bednota* (the poor peasants) were no longer unchallenged masters in the villages. Despite the prominence of this campaign at the time, it has disappeared from the present-day historian's horizon, because it does not fit into prevailing stereotypes about Bolshevism during the civil war.

Gradually Lenin worked out a new and more ambitious scenario: enlist the middle peasant directly into the socialist cause. But how? What could convince the middle peasant of the advantages of socialism? Existing models of collective agricultural production – the *kommuny* and state farms run by poor peasants – were embarrassing failures. Furthermore, the use of violence to transform production relations was a non-option. This point needs to be brought out, precisely because there was a lot of state violence against the peasantry during the civil war, both to extract needed resources and to crush peasant rebels. But these traditional forms of state violence were sharply distinguished in Lenin's mind – and

Lenin is fascinated by a presentation of an electric plough, a new way of demonstrating the advantages of socialism to the peasants (October 1921).

no doubt in peasant consciousness as well – from violence used to transform production methods. From a Marxist point of view coercing people to adopt a higher form of production was not so much wrong as absurd.

As he watched his hopes for state farms and *kommuny* crumble Lenin only became *more* insistent on the inadmissibility of using force – a fundamental contrast with Stalin. Precisely in 1919, at the height of the civil war, we find Lenin's most emphatic pronouncements on this subject. 'Before anything else, we must base ourselves on this truth: violent methods will achieve nothing here, due to the very essence of the matter . . . *There is nothing more stupid than the very idea of violence in the area of property relations of the middle peasantry.*'[36] 'The absurdity of [any use of violence to install *kommuny*] is so obvious that the Soviet government long ago forbade it'. Soon 'the last trace of this outrage [*bezobrazie*] will be swept from the face of the Soviet Republic'.[37]

Lenin finally decided that the advantages of socialism would be demonstrated to the middle peasants, not directly by collective experiments within the village, but indirectly. Instead of propagating 'oases of collective production' in the petty-bourgeois desert, the new path to socialist transformation in the countryside would rely on the transforming power of socialist industry. In January 1920, at the height of his disillusionment with *sovkhozy* and *kommuny*, Lenin read an article by the Bolshevik engineer Gleb Krzhizhanovsky on the vast potential of Russia's electrification. Lenin himself was electrified: here was a way out of his dilemma. For him, the plan for electrification represented 'a second party program' (symbolically taking the place of the aborted 'second October'). This new peasant strategy is the inner meaning of Lenin's famous slogan from late 1920: 'Communism is soviet power plus electrification of the whole country.'[38]

Another and even more direct way of way of revealing the advantages of socialism was providing the peasants with equipment, clothing, medical supplies and other necessary items *through state channels*. As with the issue of violence, a common misunderstanding makes it imperative to stress that *even during the civil war* Lenin insisted on the need to provide material incentives to the countryside. He hardly needed to wait for NEP to realize this. Of course, during the civil war, material items to exchange with the peasants were far and few between:

August 1919: It's not hard to understand that the workers' government cannot now give the peasant goods, because industry is at a standstill. There's no bread, no fuel, no industry. Every reasonable peasant will agree that it is necessary to give his surplus grain to the starving worker as a loan to be paid off by industrial items.[39]

March 1920: The imperialist war and then the war against counter-revolution, however, have laid waste to and ruined the entire country. We must bend all efforts to conquer the chaos, to restore industry and agriculture, and to give the peasants the goods they need in exchange for grain.[40]

Lenin and the Bolsheviks promised to provide the peasants with exchange items, but they wanted to provide these goods via state channels. Lenin admitted that the state organs of distribution still had many defects 'of which the workers' government is very well aware, but which cannot be eliminated in the first period of the transition to socialism'.[41] Nevertheless, Lenin looked forward to steady progress toward genuinely socialist distribution. Hostilities would cease, industry would revive and the socialist state would get its act together by improving its own organizations.

The decriminalization of the private grain trade in 1921 ended this scenario of steady progress toward socialist distribution. The reliance on long-term projects such as electrification also meant that socialist transformation of the countryside had to be put on hold. In spring 1921 Lenin justified the introduction of NEP by remarking that 'as long as we have not remade [the peasant], as long as large-scale machinery has not remade him, we have to assure him the possibility of being his own boss'.[42] The key economic link between town and country was no longer the state, but once again the market and the private merchant. This was indeed a severe setback, a retreat on the road to socialism. Therefore, in one of his final articles, Lenin urged his readers not to forget about the original project of using state-controlled channels such as the cooperatives to gradually crowd out private trade.[43]

NEP did not change Lenin's strategy for enlisting the support of the middle peasant for socialism – it merely changed the dimensions of the problem. The basic goal remained, as before, to provide abundant material goods through state channels. Before NEP, the enemy to be overcome was the pervasive underground market. After NEP, it was the decriminalized private grain market – the same enemy, with a different legal status.

Lenin's strategy can be labelled the *kto-kovo* scenario. This label may strike some readers as paradoxical, because the phrase *kto-kovo*, or 'who-whom', has entered educated folklore as Lenin's favourite phrase and an expression of his essentially hard-line outlook. 'Who-whom' is therefore usually glossed as something on the order of 'who shall destroy whom?' In reality Lenin only used the phrase two or three times at the very end of his career, and even then did not give it any prominence. If *kto-kovo* had not been picked up, first by Zinoviev and then by other Bolshevik leaders, the phrase would have been long forgotten. *Kto-kovo* was adopted as a pithy expression of the logic of NEP – not usually considered Lenin at his most hard-line.[44] The phrase should be glossed as something like the following: 'which class will succeed in winning the loyalty of the peasants: the proletariat or the now-tolerated bourgeoisie (the so-called *nepman*)?' Although Lenin only let drop the phrase *kto-kovo* a couple of off-hand times, he expressed often and forcefully the scenario to which the term later became attached. Perhaps the most eloquent version is found in the concluding words of one of his last articles:

> In the final analysis, the fate of our republic will depend on whether the peasant masses will stand by the working class, loyal to their alliance, or whether they will permit the 'nepmen', that is, the new bourgeoisie, to drive a wedge between them and the working class, to create a schism between them and the working class. The more clearly we see this alternative, the more clearly all our workers and peasants understand it, the greater are the chances that we shall avoid a schism that would be fatal for the Soviet republic.[45]

The *nepman* or new bourgeoisie had now replaced the liberal bourgeoisie in the role of rival leadership. Although *kto-kovo* was a late coinage to express what Lenin saw as the class logic of NEP, it also reflected the basic logic of Lenin's heroic scenario. The *kto-kovo* scenario is the Old Bolshevik scenario dusted off and applied to the realities of NEP.

And so it appears that Lenin came up with a new scenario that still reflected the optimistic spirit of his original one of inspiring class leadership. But the adjustment did not come without cost. As in the case of international revolution, the new scenario had a built-in anxiety factor that had previously been absent. One of Lenin's fundamental axioms had always been that individual small-scale production for the market will inevitably give rise to full-scale capitalism. This axiom was not a source of anxiety for the original Old Bolshevik scenario. On the contrary, capitalist transformation of Russia was seen as a progressive factor, creating indefatigable fighters for the democratic revolution and later for the socialist revolution. But circumstances had altered. Now the capitalism created by the 'petty-bourgeois peasantry' was a threat to steady steps to socialism and therefore to the whole legitimacy of socialist revolution in Russia.

Lenin expressed this anxiety with great intensity after 1919. It shows up in his diatribes against 'free trade' during the civil war. The amorphous but mighty force of peasant capitalism was fighting a war against the grain monopoly – and in so doing it was condemning the cities to starvation. As he expostulated in the summer of 1920:[46]

> The abolition of classes not only means driving out the landlords and capitalists – something we accomplished with comparative ease – it means *abolishing the small commodity producers* [= those who produce for the market], and they *cannot be driven out; we must live* in harmony *them; they can (and must) by remoulded and re-educated only by very prolonged, slow, cautious organizational work.*
>
> They encircle the proletariat on every side with a petty-bourgeois atmosphere, which permeates and corrupts the proletariat

and causes constant relapses among the proletariat into petty-bourgeois spinelessness, disunity, individualism, and alternate moods of exaltation and dejection . . . Millions of millions of small producers, by their ordinary, everyday, imperceptible, elusive, demoralizing activity achieve the *very* results which the bourgeoisie need and which *restore* the bourgeoisie.[47]

The retreat associated with NEP only intensified this anxiety. Lenin's obsessing about the abstract force of 'petty-bourgeois individual production' sits uneasily next to his optimistic hopes for class leadership of the middle peasant. Yet both have deep roots in his life-long heroic scenario.

The Cultural Deficit

In late 1920 Lenin's long-time associate Grigory Zinoviev recalled the hopes placed in 1917 on 'soviet democracy'. The democratically elected soviets were supposed to be 'organs in which the creativity of the masses finds for itself the most free and most organized path, the soviets as organs that guaranteed a constant stream of fresh forces from below, the soviets as organs where the masses learned at one and the same time to legislate and to carry out their own laws'.[48] Zinoviev contrasted these dreams with the bleak reality that by late 1920 'the most elementary demands of democratism' were being ignored.[49]

The disappointing record of the soviets as instruments of democratic renewal had one implication that increasingly preoccupied Lenin. The soviets were supposed to abolish 'bureaucratism' and to completely remake the inherited state apparatus. But as Lenin became more and more frustrated in his dealings with the state bureaucracy he was forced to search for new ways to combat pervasive bureaucratism.

By 1922 Lenin's anger about the deficiencies of the state bureaucracy had become an obsession. As he remarked to a colleague in February 1922, 'departments are shit, decrees are shit. Find people, check up on work – these are everything'.[50] All through the year he continued to excoriate the *gosapparat* (state apparatus) and to trace all its inefficiencies and failures to the original sin of tsarism. Again and again Lenin worries that the party is not controlling the state machinery, but the other way around. The state machinery was 'like a car that was going not in the direction the driver desired, but in the direction someone else desired; as if it were being driven by some mysterious, lawless hand, God knows whose, perhaps of a profiteer, or of a private capitalist, or of both.'[51]

As these remarks show the bureaucracy had become a third source of anxiety, alongside the encirclements by international capitalism and by the 'petty-bourgeois' peasantry. The new enemy acquired a bitterly ironical label: the 'soviet bureaucrat'. Back in 1917 this term would have appeared absurdly oxymoronic, since the soviets were viewed as the polar opposite of 'bureaucratism'. But after 1917 'the soviets' became more and more of a synonym for the state apparatus as distinct from the party. Just like the pre-revolutionary bureaucracy, the personnel of the 'soviet apparatus' was made up mainly of middle-class 'bourgeois specialists'. They were automatically assumed to be hostile to the socialist cause, or perhaps even saboteurs. Lenin now referred to the soviet bureaucracy as a haven for the shattered remnants of the capitalists and landowners.

Why had the soviets failed so signally that they had almost turned into their opposite? Lenin's diagnosis focused on the cultural deficit of the proletariat and (even more) the *narod*. Lenin used *kultura* to mean such things as literacy, elementary habits of organization and other basic skills of modern 'civilization' (another term frequently found in his late writings). The cultural level of the 'soviet bureaucracy' was also very low, according to Lenin. Yet,

Russia's new elite: a provincial party committee in Perm, 1922.

worryingly, these bureaucrats had more culture than the workers or even the Communists. Lenin compared the Bolsheviks to barbarians who had conquered a higher civilization. Didn't history show the very real danger that 'the vanquished nation imposes its culture upon the conqueror', that is, 'Communists stand at the head of departments, enjoying rank and title, but actually swimming with the stream together with the bourgeoisie'?[52]

The cultural deficit explained the failure of Lenin's hopes for the soviets, but it also posed a direct challenge to the legitimacy of socialist revolution in backward Russia. Lenin was confronted by this challenge in January 1923 when he read a memoir of the 1917 revolution written by the left-wing socialist Nikolai Sukhanov. In notes dictated soon afterwards Lenin admitted that socialist critics such as Sukhanov had correctly asserted that Russia was not ready for socialism. He responded to these familiar arguments with a flood of rhetorical questions (I count nine in two pages).

Such questions are the rhetorical device of choice for those who are not quite sure of their position. Lenin's questions boil down to two: weren't we justified in taking power in 1917 by Russia's otherwise hopeless situation? Who's to say we can't pull off the unexpected task of creating cultural prerequisites for socialism *after* taking power?[53]

Lenin's defensive tone shows his uneasy awareness that there was something deeply unorthodox about this relation between a proletarian *vlast* and culture. The standard Marxist schema proposed the following sequence:

capitalism $\rightarrow$ culture $\rightarrow$ *vlast* $\rightarrow$ socialism

For Russia at least, Lenin now maintained that the following sequence was permissible and indeed necessary:

capitalism $\rightarrow$ *vlast* $\rightarrow$ culture $\rightarrow$ socialism

In Marxist terms, the idea of the proletarian *vlast* creating the cultural basis for its own successful existence bears a resemblance to the way Baron Munchausen pulled himself out of the mire by his own bootstraps.

Lenin needed something like a miracle, so he again evoked the spirit of *What Is to Be Done?*, the book in which he boasted that an ordinary underground activist, even in isolation, could achieve miracles if he embodied the spirit of inspired and inspiring leadership. We shall look at two of Lenin's attempts to put this spirit to work for the revolution, one in 1919 at the height of the civil war, and the other in 1923, now in a considerably chastened form.

In early 1919 the Bolshevik leader Jacob Sverdlov died of typhus. Sverdlov was the organization man of the Bolshevik top staff and his death was a real blow to the efficient running of the party. Lenin's eulogy for him was the occasion for a classic exposition of his own concept of leadership. In his eulogy Lenin insists that repressive violence, seen by many people as the essence of Bolshevism, was only an enforced necessity. The real essence of Bolshevism was inspired and inspiring class leadership or, as he expresses it here, Bolshevism's ability to organize the proletariat and through it the *narod*. A party leader (*vozhd*) such as Sverdlov can organize the masses because his utter devotion to the cause gives him 'moral authority'. Sverdlov was only the most outstanding of a whole corps of *vozhdi* 'pushed forward' by the proletariat from its own ranks. According to Lenin these proletarian leaders had started to replace intelligentsia leaders around the beginning of the century.

As so often when discussing heroic leadership, Lenin alluded covertly to the fate of his brother, who had been tragically deprived of the opportunity to become such a leader:

> The history of the Russian revolutionary movement over the course of many decades has known a long list of people, devoted to the revolutionary cause, but who did not enjoy the possibility of finding a practical application of their revolutionary ideals. And, in this connection, the proletarian revolution was the first to give these previously isolated individuals, heroes of the revolutionary struggle, a genuine grounding, a genuine base, a genuine framework, a genuine audience and a genuine prole-tarian army, where these *vozhdi* could reveal themselves.[54]

The image of the proletariat as an 'audience' for the inspiring leader – an image also found in *What Is to Be Done?* – brings out the unique quality of Lenin's heroic scenario.

In his final articles of early 1923 Lenin once again calls upon the aid of proletarian leaders who arise directly from the working class, but now in a much smaller and more prosaic context. The grand vistas of the civil war have receded and Lenin now calls on recruits from the working class to improve the working of the state

At the unveiling of a statue to Marx and Engels, November 1918: Lenin next to Jacob Sverdlov (Lenin's model of inspiring leadership).

administrative machinery. The institutional details of his scheme are less important to us than its reliance on class leadership in yet another guise. Just as in *What Is to Be Done?* Lenin's 1923 plan was to recruit up-and-coming workers from the bench into responsible posts in the party organization, with the same expectation that this infusion will make the party unbeatable.[55]

But Lenin was now determined to keep the whole process under control. The task previously given to the masses, acting through the soviets, is now handed to the party, acting from above: 'We still have the old machinery, and our task now is to remould it along new lines. We cannot do so at once, but we must see to it that the Communists we have are properly placed . . . Our party, a little group of people in comparison with the country's total population, has tackled this job. This tiny nucleus has set itself the task of remaking everything, and it will do so.'[56]

Despite the contrived and mundane nature of the organizational scheme propagated in his final articles, Lenin invested it with his

usual emotional fervour. In 1902 he wrote about his scheme for
an underground newspaper: 'That is what we must dream about!'
In 1923 he wrote about his scheme to improve state administrative
machinery: 'These are the lofty tasks I dream of for our Rabkrin
[Worker and Peasant Inspection].'[57]

Lenin's Rabkrin scheme was an attempt to overcome the cultural
deficit that Lenin blamed for the deficiencies of the soviet bureaucracy. It has the air of a desperate improvization, an attempt to
square the circle, and as such it was never remotely practicable.
But the other prong of Lenin's attack on the cultural deficit was
much more substantive: mass education for the *narod*. We might
call this Lenin's *kukharka* strategy, after his famous boast in 1917
that the Bolsheviks would teach the *kukharka*, the female cook,
how to administer the state.

In 'Pages from a Diary', the most eloquent of Lenin's final articles
– and one that has not received the attention it deserves – we see
for the last time Ilich, son of Ilya Ulyanov, the tsarist educational
reformer. After going through some statistics showing Russia's low
literacy, Lenin insists that education of the *narod* must be made a top
priority. The country must make a real shift in budgetary priorities
toward education, particularly by improving the material position
of the schoolteacher of the *narod*. The status of the schoolteacher
should be higher in Soviet Russia than in any bourgeois society.

True to his lifelong scenario, Lenin sees the 'gigantic, world-
historical cultural task' of mass education in terms of class leadership, as drawing the peasant 'away from union with the bourgeoisie
and toward union with the proletariat'. At the end of his career
Lenin once again summoned up the ultimate guarantor of his
'other way': the Russian people on the move, transformed by
the pressures of modernity, eager to liquidate the heritage of
pre-modern backwardness, or, as Lenin put it, the 'semi-asiatic
absence of culture':

We are speaking of the semi-asiatic absence of culture, from which we have not yet extricated ourselves, and from which we cannot extricate ourselves without strenuous effort – although certainly the possibility exists of our doing so, because nowhere are the masses of the *narod* so interested in real culture as they are in our country; nowhere are the problems of culture posed so profoundly and consistently as they are in our country; in no other country is the state *vlast* in the hands of the working class which, in its mass, is fully aware of the deficiencies, I shall not say of its culture, but of its literacy; nowhere is the working class so ready to make, and nowhere is it actually making, such sacrifices to improve its position in this respect as in our country.[58]

Lenin's Final Year

Lenin's attempts to move beyond the 'textbook à la Kautsky' took its toll. From 1919 his speeches lose their earlier sharpness and become progressively more unfocused, repetitive, digressive. He becomes defensive and halting as he searches for a way to match his ideological scenario with events. A new and unexpected quality appears: Lenin is unsure of himself.

Nevertheless, in his articles published in January 1923 Lenin strove to achieve at least a provisional synthesis. The result is an idiosyncratic blend of anxiety and confidence. Lenin could not really abandon the axioms of the textbook à la Kautsky even when they challenged the legitimacy of socialism in Soviet Russia. Among these axioms are the following: Only a series of revolutions in the advanced countries will crush capitalism. A successful fight for socialism in Russia requires the dissolution of the peasantry into bourgeoisie and proletariat. Small-scale production for the market engenders capitalism. The proletariat will achieve socialism on the basis of the cultural achievements of capitalism. Lenin believed

Lenin fades away, but the new elite remains (one of Lenin's last public appearances, October 1922).

in these axioms all his life, and he couldn't stop believing them simply because they had become inconvenient. As a result Lenin saw the Bolsheviks encircled by three founts of anxiety: international capitalism, the 'petty-bourgeois' peasantry and the dubiously loyal 'soviet bureaucrat'.

Even so, Lenin looked to the future with confidence, on the basis of an adjusted version of his heroic scenario. If by 'Lenin's testament', we mean his final message to the party, it can be summarized as follows:

Hopes have faded for socialist revolution in Europe anytime in the foreseeable future? Then take courage from the inevitable awakening of the East, while praying that inter-capitalist squabbles will allow socialist Russia to hold out.

Hopes have faded that the peasants would move toward socialist transformation on their own initiative? Then take the Old Bolshevik scenario of class leadership that had vindicated itself during the civil war and apply it to the novel task of leading the 'middle peasant' to socialism.

Hopes have faded that soviet-style democracy from below will transform the state? Then use the party to remake the inherited state apparatus from above, and put the highest possible priority on campaigns for mass literacy.

Do all these faded hopes mean that our socialist critics were right and that Russia was not ready for socialism? Yes, but – who's to say that a proletarian *vlast* cannot pull itself up by its own bootstraps by itself creating the cultural prerequisites for socialism?

Lenin's final stroke on 6 March 1923 marks the real end-point of his life and work, although his physical death came almost a year later. During the rest of 1923 Lenin was barely able to communicate. A moving description of Lenin's state during this period comes from a letter from Yevgeny Preobrazhensky to Bukharin, describing a visit to Lenin in July 1923:

I had just come downstairs with Belenkii [Lenin's security guard], when in the room to the right of the entrance Belenkii gestured with his arm toward the window: 'over there, they're carrying him'. When about twenty-five feet away he noticed me, to our horror, and started to press his hand to his chest and shouting 'over there, there' – asking for me. I had just come and had not yet seen M. I. and N. K. [Maria Ulyanova and Krupskaya]. They came running, and M. I., quite upset, said 'since he's noticed you, you have to go to him'.

I went, not exactly knowing how to behave or even, really, whom I would see. I decided to keep a happy and cheerful face at all times. I approached him. He pressed my hand firmly, I instinctively embraced him. But his face! It cost me a great effort to keep my mask and not to cry like a baby. In this face there was so much suffering, but not only the sufferings of the present moment. It was as if on his face were photographed and frozen all the sufferings he had undergone during this whole period.[59]

The final stroke occurred on 21 January 1924. An hour after, Vladimir Ilich Ulyanov, known to the world as N. Lenin, breathed his last.

Epilogue

The highly emotional link between the flesh-and-blood individual Vladimir Ulyanov and his public persona N. Lenin consisted of a heroic scenario that gave content and meaning to his statistical investigations, his incessant polemics, his political strategies and all other aspects of his career. The basic contours of this heroic scenario were set out by Lenin in St Petersburg in 1893–4 and remained unchanged for the rest of his life.

Lenin's scenario can be compressed into a single sentence or expanded into three hundred pages on capitalist development in Russia. The one-sentence version goes something like this: The Russian proletariat carries out its world historical mission by becoming the *vozhd* of the *narod*, leading a revolution that over-throws the tsar and institutes political freedom, thus preparing the ground for an eventual proletarian *vlast* that will bring about socialism. What propels this drama forward is inspired and inspir-ing class leadership. The party activists inspire the proletariat who inspire the Russian *narod* who inspire the whole world with their revolutionary feats.

The key words in the preceding summary are a mixture of learned terms imported from Europe (proletariat, revolution, socialism) and a deeply Russian vocabulary (*vozhd, narod, vlast*). I have transliterated rather than translated the key Russian words. The normal translations – *vozhd* = leader, *narod* = people, *vlast* = power – are not inaccurate, but they bleach the emotional colour out of Lenin's rhetoric. By now the reader of this book will have seen these words in a variety of contexts and will have acquired a feel for their hard-to-translate connotations.

The combination of an assertively 'scientific' terminology and a romantic narrative is brought out with almost naive frankness by one of Lenin's closest associates, Grigory Zinoviev, in a lecture on party history given in 1923:

> The advocates of 'Economism' [around the turn of the century] did not acknowledge the hegemonic role of the proletariat. They would say: 'So what, in your opinion, is the working class, a Messiah?' To this we answered and answer now: Messiah and messianism are not our language and we do not like such words; but we accept the concept that is contained in them: yes, the working class is in a certain sense a Messiah and its role is a messianic one, for this is the class which will liberate the whole world.
>
> The workers have nothing to lose but their chains; they do not have property, they sell their labour, and this is the only class which has an interest in reconstructing the world along new lines and is capable of leading the peasantry against the bourgeoisie. We avoid semi-mystical terms like Messiah and messianism and prefer the scientific one: the *hegemonic proletariat*.[1]

'Reconstructing the world' is the proletariat's mission in the general Marxist narrative, while 'leading the peasantry' is a mission much more specific to Bolshevism. Although the role of the proletariat as leader of the *narod* does have very deep roots in European Marxism, its strategic and emotional centrality is a distinctive feature of Lenin and Bolshevism.

Lenin's heroic scenario originated as a response to the dead end faced by the Russian revolutionary tradition in the 1880s. An informed British observer, writing in 1905, describes the 1880s as the Russian socialists themselves remembered it:

We thus arrive at the beginning of the eighties. Consider the situation – the People's Will Party [*Narodnaya volya*] lying on the ground broken and exhausted, reaction rampant, all that was but a short time ago hopeful, disheartened and embittered. Where shall we turn for light and guidance? To the people? It is mute. To the working-class? There is none. To the educated classes? They are all full of pessimism in the consciousness of their weakness. What, then, next? Is all hope to be given up? Is there no salvation for Russia? At this moment of darkness and despair a new and strange voice resounds through the space – a voice full of harshness and sarcasm, yet vibrating with hope. That is the voice of Russian Social-Democracy.[2]

The dilemmas of the 1880s had a meaning for Lenin that was not only political but deeply personal, since they destroyed his older brother Alexander, who lost his life in a futile attempt to move the democratic revolution forward. Alexander's fate led to Lenin's deep emotional commitment to a heroic scenario that showed him 'another way' to achieve Alexander's aims. Lenin never mentioned his brother in public. But at every stage of his career Lenin adamantly insisted that events were realizing the dream of the martyrs of the Russian revolutionary tradition.

Lenin became a passionate Social Democrat because he thought that this Western European movement showed the way forward for the Russian revolutionaries. Marxist analysis of Russia's capitalist transformation proved to him that this irresistible force was uprooting old ways of life and turning the masses of the *narod* into potential fighters for democratic rights. The Social Democratic strategy of party-led class leadership, as embodied in the German SPD, gave him a method for realizing this potential. So vast was the power generated by this combination of objective change and energetic class leadership that it could even operate under tsarist repression – in fact, it could destroy tsarism and establish the political freedom enjoyed by Western Social Democracy. What for Alexander Ulyanov had been a duel between the government and a handful of daring revolutionaries now became an epic national struggle.

Lenin's dedication to the *konspiratsiia* underground only makes sense in the context of his vision of a nationwide struggle. In contrast to the conspiratorial underground of the Russian populists the central task of the Social Democratic *konspiratsiia* underground was to get out the message. For Lenin the underground was a lever of Archimedes that greatly magnified the impact of a relatively feeble and persecuted organization. The underground could turn Russia around, because the seed it sowed fell on the fertile ground of Russia's militant workers and awakening *narod*. The party's role as inspiring class leader remained the same for Lenin even after it left the underground, even after it took power.

As shown by his rhetoric throughout his career, the emotions that Lenin invested in his scenario can only be described by such words as enthusiastic, exalted, romantic. The flip side of emotions such as these is his hatred of 'philistinism', that is, everyone and anyone who could not lift themselves up to the grand vistas of his scenario. As he wrote to Inessa Armand in 1916: 'There it is, my fate. One fighting campaign after another – against political stupidities, philistinism, opportunism and so forth. It has been going on since 1893. And so has the hatred of the philistines on account of it. But still, I would not exchange this fate for "peace" with the philistines.'[3]

His emotional commitment to his scenario also made Lenin want to base it on the most solid authority possible. This explains Lenin's love affair (the term is not too strong) with the writings of Marx and Engels. It also explains his life-long love–hate relationship with Karl Kautsky, who gave an authoritative stamp of approval to the key ideas of Old Bolshevism, but who later (as Lenin thought)

Lenin wholly focused on the effective presentation of his vision at the third
congress of the Third International, summer 1921.

failed to live up to his own preaching – thus becoming, in Lenin's
mind, the ultimate philistine and renegade.

So far we have looked at some constant themes in Lenin's outlook. We need also to consider the diversity of Lenin's concerns
throughout his career and the heroic scenario will help us out here
as well. The scenario had an internal structure of three distinct
episodes, as set forth already in the 'banner sentence' of 1894. These
episodes grow out of the basic logic of class leadership. In the first
episode the Social Democratic party is founded and becomes
accepted as leader of the proletariat. This episode is summarized
by Kautsky's foundational formula about 'the merger of socialism
and the worker movement'. In the central episode the proletariat
leads the *narod* in a crusade to overthrow the tsar, 'the shame and
curse of Russia'. In the final episode party and proletariat move
toward the climax of the drama, socialist revolution itself.

Each of the three decades of Lenin's political career matches up
neatly with one of the three episodes. The full breakdown is given

in the table overleaf. The heroic scenario thus gives us a handy device for recalling the overall contours of Lenin's career. Since the scenario was an interpretive framework for events, not a prediction of concrete outcomes, it could be mapped onto events in a variety of ways. For example, Lenin's scenario posits a rapid spread of Social Democratic influence among the workers. At any particular time a judgement call still has to be made about the actual extent of party influence. Although Lenin strove to be accurate and hard-headed in the empirical application of the Social Democratic scenario, he tended as a general rule to push for the most optimistic possible reading, up to and often past the point of plausibility.

A changed reading of the empirical situation could lead to crucial shifts of outlook. Although the goal adopted in 1917 – 'steps toward socialism' in Russia, prior to and independent of European revolution – was a far-reaching innovation in Lenin's political platform, it remained within the logic of the original scenario. Lenin had always argued that socialist revolution was only possible when class conflict within the peasantry had reached an advanced stage, but the timing of this process was explicitly left open. In 1905–7, Lenin argued that the petty bourgeois peasant was still a fervent fighter for the democratic revolution. In 1917–18, Lenin was so eager to take 'steps toward socialism' that he grossly overestimated the extent of class polarization within the village.

Only at the end of his career did Lenin make serious adjustments to his scenario. In the period following the first anniversary of the revolution – late 1918 and early 1919 – Lenin was still completely convinced that things were 'turning out just as we said they would'. The course of events soon forced him to take tentative steps beyond 'the textbook à la Kautsky', yet the basic logic of the scenario remained. Because Lenin still accepted the basic Marxist axioms that guaranteed his scenario, his adjustments caused him a great deal of anxiety and gave rise to a sense of encirclement by hostile forces such as international capitalism, petty-bourgeois peasantry

Decade	Episode Label	Banner Sentence from 1894	Central Project of the Decade
1894–1904	Social Democratic	When the advanced representatives of this class assimilate the ideas of scientific socialism and the idea of the historical role of the Russian worker – when these ideas receive a broad dissemination – when durable organizations are created among the workers that transform the present uncoordinated economic war of the workers into a purposive class struggle . . .	Creation of a Russian Social Democratic party and a functioning *konspiratsiia* underground
1904–1914	Bolshevik	. . . then the Russian WORKER, elevated to the head of all democratic elements, will overthrow absolutism . . .	Carrying out the democratic, political, anti-tsarist revolution 'to the end' by means of proletarian class leadership of the peasantry as a whole
1914–1924	Communist	. . . and lead the RUSSIAN PROLETARIAT (side by side with the proletariat of ALL COUNTRIES) by the direct road of open political struggle to THE VICTORIOUS COMMUNIST REVOLUTION.	Turn the imperialist war into a civil war for socialist revolution; establish a proletarian *vlast* in Russia that will take immediate steps toward socialism

The dramatic structure of Lenin's career.

and soviet bureaucrats. This anxiety was the result precisely of his earlier over-optimism, leading Lenin to make risky wagers that events did not justify.

Even faced with these disappointments Lenin remained loyal to the spirit of his heroic scenario and called on the power of class leadership to accomplish one more round of miracles. His final advice to the party was: hold out against international capitalism while providing an inspiring model for Eastern countries, capture the loyalty of the middle peasant by revealing the advantages of socialism, and attack the cultural deficit both indirectly and head-on. The political testament contained in his last writings is the final, somewhat chastened but still recognizable version of his heroic scenario.

Historical Impact of Lenin's Scenario

At some point after the Second World War mainstream academic scholarship took a wrong turning and became convinced that Lenin's essential trait throughout his career was 'worry about workers', coupled with a dour, if pragmatic, pessimism. Historians came close to turning Lenin into the philistine he always abominated. This basic misapprehension of Lenin's outlook made it impossible to give a coherent account of his development and his decisions at key points. The historical impact of the actual Lenin, for good or for ill, cannot be understood apart from his life-long heroic scenario.

The following brief speculative remarks should be prefaced with a disclaimer. Lenin is only a part of Bolshevism, which in turn is only a part of the Russian revolution, which in turn is only a part of the whole period of social upheaval from 1914 to 1921–2 that many Russians term a 'time of troubles'. Furthermore, much of Lenin's heroic scenario was not unique to him, but reflected much more widely held viewpoints. As a first approximation, we can say that the general theme of inspired and inspiring class leadership was a general feature of 'revolutionary Social Democracy', the theme of proletarian leadership of the *narod* ('hegemony of the proletariat') was a general feature of Bolshevism, while many of the details about class differentiation within the peasantry were peculiar to Lenin and perhaps his closest followers.

The immense cultural impact of Lenin's heroic scenario on the Soviet Union stems from the fact, first, that it was heroic and, second, that it was a scenario. The culture of the Soviet Union always put a tremendous emphasis on the heroic, although this theme was expressed in different ways over the years. The theme of heroism was embedded in an explicit dramatic scenario about the world-historical mission of the Soviet Union that was propagated at all levels. Terry Pratchett's novel *Witches Abroad* describes a somewhat similar society: a tyrannical queen forces everyone in her kingdom to act just as if they were characters in the canonical fairy tales. In the case of the Soviet Union and other communist countries a similar tyranny of narrative expectations met with a particular kind of resistance: the *anekdot*, the Soviet joke, whose specific flavour comes from subverting a heroic scenario. Socialist realism and the *anekdot*: these two poles of Soviet culture both stem from the heroic scenario.[4]

One feature of Lenin's heroic scenario that had an immense if underappreciated impact is what I have called the *kukharka* strategy: mass education for both men and women. I have explained the personal origin of this theme by pointing to Lenin's popular nickname Ilich, son of Ilya, the educational reformer. But since the insistence on equal educational opportunity from both sexes goes back to both of Lenin's parents, I should also speak of Lenin the son of Maria Aleksandrovna, as well as Lenin the brother of Anna and Maria, the husband of Nadezhda and the friend of Inessa. The economic consequences of the *kukharka* strategy are illuminated in a recent analysis by the economist Robert C. Allen. Before the Russian revolution Russia had the same non-European demographic pattern as, say, India: high death rate, high birth rate. Yet the Soviet Union did not have the same population explosion as India, with immense consequences for economic growth. The demographic disasters of the Soviet era – the civil war, the famines, the repressions and the Second World War – played an appreciable but not major impact in preventing this explosion. The main reason was a dramatically fast drop in the birth rate, and comparative analysis shows that the education of women was the key factor in this achievement. Allen concludes that 'if industrialization and urbanization had proceeded less rapidly and if schooling had been expanded slowly and provided to men in preference to women, then population growth would have been explosive'.[5]

When we turn to the political impact of Lenin's heroic scenario, we are immediately confronted with a paradox. The central episode of the heroic scenario was the battle to bring political freedom to Russia, yet Lenin founded a regime in which political freedoms – rights of speech, assembly, association, etc. – were conspicuously absent. The paradox is a real one, since the logic of the heroic scenario worked to expand Russia's political freedom at one stage and to contract it at another. Strange as it may appear, Lenin was as influential as any other single individual in bringing about the political freedom that Russia enjoyed between 1905 and 1917. There would have been no far-reaching revolution in 1905 if sections of the working class had not been prepared to take to the streets demanding political freedom, and there would have been no mass action of this kind if a small band of socialists had not spent over a decade propagating the connection between worker interests, socialist ideals and political freedom. From the very beginning of his political career, Lenin was a prominent and passionate member of this small band.

There are many objective reasons to explain the later failure of political freedom in a country that suffered military defeat, economic breakdown and bloody civil war. Yet although the disappearance of political freedom in Russia was over-determined, the logic of Lenin's heroic scenario also made its contribution. The purpose of political freedom in this scenario was to allow the Social Democrats to spread the word, particularly in the form of the party-led agitation campaigns that the German Social Democrats had developed to a fine art. How much more effective would these campaigns be if the party could use the state to eliminate all rivals and to monopolize channels of communication? The Bolsheviks consciously adopted this strategy of state monopoly campaignism.

Turning from Lenin's strangely divided role in the history of political freedom in Russia, we confront another paradoxical outcome. Lenin's heroic scenario stressed proletarian leadership of a *narod* that was made up mainly of peasants. The peasants thus play a highly positive role in his scenario. Indeed, pre-war Old Bolshevism was defined by its wager on the revolutionary qualities of the peasantry. Yet less than a decade after his death the regime founded by Lenin ended up by waging war on the peasants and imposing a revolution from above during the collectivization campaign, contributing to a devastating famine. How did this happen?

This is the question of questions, and I can only glance at it here. Perhaps the most important point to stress is that it *is* a question – that is, Stalin's peasant strategy was not the foreordained outcome of a hostility to peasants innate to Marxism or to Bolshevism. In fact, we can say that Lenin took a dangerous step when he moved beyond Old Bolshevism's strategy of democratic revolution alongside the whole peasantry. He first overestimated the extent of class differentiation in order to be able to take 'steps toward socialism' in Russia itself. He then had to recalibrate and he came up with a strategy of moving toward socialism alongside a majority of the peasantry. The cost of this adjustment was an abiding anxiety, even paranoia, about the subversive influence of the vast 'petty bourgeois' sea that surrounded the lonely socialist island.

Nevertheless, there is an essential discontinuity between Lenin and Stalin on the peasant question that needs to be stressed, since it is often completely overlooked, even denied. Stalin obviously took over a vision of a socialist countryside from Lenin and indeed from Marxist socialism in general. We may agree or disagree with this vision. But from the point of view both of crimes against humanity and impact on Soviet history, the thing to be explained is not this vision, but the massive use of violence in 1930–34 to impose upon the peasantry a radical change of production methods, and thus of way of life, in a very short space of time.

And on the issue of violence used to impose a fundamental change in production relations, the record could not be clearer: Lenin was against it. In word and deed he emphasized that any such use of violence was a *bezobrazie*, a ridiculous outrage. And he did this most insistently in 1919, at the height of the civil war. Disappointed as he was with the progress of socialist experiments in the countryside, the use of violence in pursuit of this goal was simply not considered. The radical discontinuity between Lenin and Stalin on this cardinal point was perfectly evident to anti-Stalin Bolsheviks in 1932. In an underground document circulated at this time, these Bolsheviks contrast Stalin's assault on the peasantry to Lenin's method of persuading the peasants by 'genuine examples of the genuine advantages of collective farms organized in genuinely voluntary fashion'. They sardonically observe that the two methods resembled each other as much as Japan's invasion of Manchuria resembled national self-determination.[6]

All in all, Lenin's heroic scenario was far from realistic. Yet perhaps his utter confidence in it was the necessary illusion that enabled him to confront a situation of stormy political and economic collapse. In 1917 Lenin stood tall among the leaders of other Russian parties because they had enough sense to be frightened out of their wits by the oncoming disaster – the social and economic breakdown that was just around the corner – whereas he saw it as

Lenin talking with a Moscow party official in 1920.

an opportunity. Lenin can be viewed as a Noah figure, confidently building his ark as the flood waters rose. As it turned out, the ark was leaky because it was built on unsound assumptions, the voyage involved more suffering than anyone bargained for, and the ark ended up far from where its builder planned. But nevertheless the ark did ride out the storm.

Character Witnesses

I have described the heroic scenario as the link between the flesh-and-blood individual Vladimir Ulyanov and his public persona N. Lenin. This division is of course highly artificial. To give a sense of the human reality of Ulyanov/Lenin, I call on a series of character witnesses – people with some personal knowledge of the man and of the social background that moulded him.

Lenin had strong roots in the Russian literary classics of the nineteenth century, and we can appropriately turn to them for more insight into what might be called 'the Lenin type'. Lenin always kept with him the photographs of five individuals: Karl Marx, Friedrich Engels, Alexander Herzen, Nikolai Chernyshevky and Dmitri Pisarev. Pisarev was a radical democratic literary critic of the 1860s, and Lenin cited a passage from him about the necessity of dreaming in his 1902 book *What Is to Be Done?* The following passage was *not* quoted by Lenin – perhaps because it was too close to his self-image?

> The dreamer himself sees in his dream a great and sacred truth; and he works, works conscientiously and with full strength, for his dream to stop being just a dream. His whole life is arranged according to one guiding idea and it is filled with the most strenuous activity. He is happy, despite deprivations and unpleasantness, despite the jeers of unbelievers

and despite the difficulties of struggling with deeply rooted ways of thought.[7]

Pisarev's stubborn dreamer was an admired type in the culture of Russian radicalism. In order to qualify, Lenin did not need to live the ascetic, self-denying life of such heroes of Russian socialist fiction as Chernyshevky's Rakhmetov, who slept on a bed of nails to toughen himself up. Lenin once remarked to Gorky that listening to Beethoven made him feel too soft toward the bourgeoisie who could create such beautiful things. Based on this remark, many people have assumed that Lenin gave up music for revolution, but Lenin enjoyed music all his life. When the great Russian bass Feodor Chaliapin met Lenin in the Kremlin after the revolution, he was surprised to learn that this was not their first meeting. Lenin reminded him of a party at Gorky's in 1905 when Chaliapin sang for the company. 'It was a marvellous evening', Lenin reminisced.[8]

Lenin's personal lifestyle was rather the stripped-down, orderly, no-frills style of his own ideal 'revolutionary by trade'. His attitude toward food is emblematic. The Canadian historian Carter Elwood has investigated this topic and concluded that Lenin just didn't care about food – as long as there was some on his plate, he ate it without complaint.[9]

Another, much more sardonic, take on the type of the stubborn dreamer comes from Lev Tolstoy's late novel *Resurrection*. This novel was published in 1900 and paints a devastating portrait of a morally bankrupt Russia. Toward the end of the novel, we meet some political prisoners on their way to Siberia. Tolstoy rather likes these political prisoners – except for their acknowledged leader, one Novodvorov:

> The whole of Novodvorov's revolutionary activity, though he could explain it very eloquently and very convincingly, appeared to be founded on nothing but ambition and the

desire for supremacy. Being devoid of those moral and aesthetic qualities which call forth doubts and hesitation, he very soon acquired a position in the revolutionary world which satisfied him – that of leader of a party. Having once chosen a direction, he never doubted or hesitated, and was therefore certain that he never made a mistake . . . His self-assurance was so great that it either repelled people or made them submit to him. And as he carried on his activity among very young people who mistook his boundless self-assurance for depth and wisdom, the majority did submit to him and he had great success in revolutionary circles.

Novodvorov behaved well only to those who bowed before him. He couldn't stand anyone who had his own independent analysis of Russia's ills.[10]

Those who knew Lenin tended to see him either as Pisarev's heroic dreamer or Tolstoy's petty despot, although most of the witnesses I will cite are somewhat nuanced in their judgements. Georgy Solomon (in whose Brussels apartment Lenin gave the late-night harangue about 'recallism' described in chapter Three) was strongly repelled by Lenin's 'impenetrable self-satisfaction'. Nevertheless, he was ready to qualify his dislike by adding that when Lenin was not in attack mode, 'then before you stood an intelligent and broadly educated man, highly erudite, and distinguished by a fair amount of quick-wittedness'.[11]

Alexander Bogdanov also tried to explain Lenin's puzzling combination of breadth and narrowness. Bogdanov was a top Bolshevik leader until he was forced out of the faction in 1909. In 1914 he wrote a long, unpublished critique of Lenin's mental style. He tells us that when Lenin 'investigated a specific pheno-menon, for example, the class composition and character of this or that party, he carries out the task, sometimes brilliantly'. But in larger questions Lenin's way of thinking was much too rigid:

Capri, 1908: Lenin plays chess with Alexander Bogdanov with Gorky looking on; according to Gorky's later account, Lenin lost the match.

he took over a framework from European experience and applied it to Russia come hell or high water. This intellectual rigidity and authoritarian manner of thinking meant that Lenin was prone to misinterpret a genuinely novel situation, for example, Russia after the 1905 revolution.[12]

Nikolai Sukhanov – the author of the memoir of 1917 that occasioned Lenin's 1923 article on the cultural deficit – tried to pin down his own impression of Lenin by making a comparison with Lev Tolstoy: both (writes Sukhanov) were true geniuses in certain very narrow areas, yet they each had 'no understanding or grasp of the simplest and most generally accessible things' outside of that area.[13]

The combination of narrowness of mind and complete assurance gave rise to the abusive polemical style that appalled so many who had to deal with Lenin. Writing to his close friend Nadezhda Kristi in early 1917 the Menshevik leader L. Martov explains why he is happy to think that there is no life after death: 'In my opinion, one earthly existence is more than enough: do you think it would be *drôle* to continue polemicizing with Lenin even after death and to continue to listen to his gutter abuse?'[14]

The same abusive style could be described, in an admiring way, as evidence of 'intellectual passion'. Russian émigré Moishe Olgin, writing in 1919, describes Lenin in action:

> Lenin does not reply to an opponent. He vivisects him. He is as keen as the edge of a razor. His mind works with an amazing acuteness. He notices every flaw in the line of argument. He disagrees with, and he draws the most absurd conclusions from, premises unacceptable to him. At the same time he is derisive. He ridicules his opponent. He castigates him. He makes you feel that his victim is an ignoramus, a fool, a presumptuous nonentity. You are swept by the power of his logic. You are overwhelmed by his intellectual passion.[15]

The novelist Maxim Gorky knew Lenin quite well and also had mixed feelings that varied over time. In 1920 Gorky was even ready to talk about Lenin's saintliness! In 1909, however, he wrote a rather harsh letter to Lenin. The letter contained compliments ('You are someone who I find organically sympathetic'), but also a critique based on Hamlet's metaphor of playing on someone like a recorder:

> Sometimes it seems to me that for you every person is no more than a recorder on which you play this or that melody pleasing to you – that you evaluate each person's individuality from the point of view of how useful they are to you, for the realization of your aims, opinions, tasks. This way of evaluating people (leaving to one side its profoundly individualist and elitist

underlay) necessarily creates a void around you – and while this is not so important in itself, you are a strong character – but the main thing is, this way of evaluating people will surely lead you into making mistakes.[16]

Gorky was repelled by Lenin's instrumental attitude to the people around him. Lenin's close associates understood this feature of Lenin's personality, but they interpreted it in a different way. Zinoviev, looking back in the early 1930s, wrote that Lenin had an *oshchushchenie* about his personal mission, that is, a strong 'feeling' bordering on physical sensation:

> Was there 'egocentrism' in Ilich? No.
>   Were there any dictatorial leanings? No.
>   But was there an awareness (feeling) that *he* was called? *Yes,* this there was! Without that he would not have become Lenin. Without that (precisely a strong feeling), there would be no *vozhd* at all.
>   At one time (when V. I. was still fighting for recognition), someone's relation to him personally (or rather, not 'personally,' but politically and theoretically) was for him a *criterion,* a measure of things. Only we can't understand this in a vulgar fashion.[17]

The hero-worshipping attitude to Lenin that existed even before the Bolshevik revolution comes out in a description of Lenin written in 1917 by Nikolai Bukharin, who knew Lenin well. For followers like Bukharin, Lenin himself was the ultimate inspired and inspiring leader:

> The Russian and international proletariat has found themselves a worthy *vozhd* in the person of Lenin. A veteran revolutionary, Lenin was christened on the path of revolution by the blood of

The iconic Lenin in 1919.

his own brother, hanged by the butcher Alexander III. And hatred toward the oppressors took deep root in his soul. Lenin has a highly analytical mind and yet at the same time he is a person of iron will, always travelling the path that he considers the correct one. He is equally firm when he must swim almost alone 'against the current' and when he needs to work in the midst of his own people. Revolution is his element. He is a genuine *vozhd* of the revolution, following out his own logic to the end, scourging any half-heartedness, any refusal to draw conclusions.[18]

We have summoned character witnesses both friendly and hostile to Lenin, but a certain mystery will always remain. An emblem of this mystery is Lenin's characteristic laugh. Two visiting

Lenin, accompanied by his sister Maria, hurries along a Moscow street to attend a meeting in 1918; on the wall is a poster for a recital by Feodor Chaliapin.

Englishmen, interviewing Lenin in 1919 and 1920, reacted to this laugh in different ways:

> *Arthur Ransome*: 'This little bald-headed, wrinkled man, who tilts his chair this way and that, laughing over one thing or another, ready any minute to give serious advice to any who interrupt him to ask for it, advice so well reasoned that it is to his followers far more compelling than any command, every one of his wrinkles is a wrinkle of laughter, not of worry.'[19]

> *Bertrand Russell*: 'He is very friendly, and apparently simple, entirely without a trace of *hauteur* . . . I have never met a personage so destitute of self-importance . . . . He laughs a great deal; at first his laugh seems merely friendly and jolly, but gradually I came to feel it rather grim.'[20]

We end by repeating the words of Lenin's widow, Nadezhda Krupskaya, who provided the Ariadne's thread that has guided us through the labyrinth of Lenin's career. She first met Lenin in St Petersburg in 1894. It was here, she tells us, that Lenin fully committed himself to what he saw as 'Marx's grand idea': 'only as *vozhd* of all the labourers will the working class achieve victory'. Once Lenin made this commitment, he never wavered: 'this thought, this idea illuminated all of his later activity, each and every step.'

References

Introduction

1 L. Kamenev, 'The Literary Legacy and Collected Works of Ilyitch' (written in the early 1920s), text taken from Marxists Internet Archive, www.marxists.org/archive/kamenev/19xx/x01/x01.htm (accessed 5 May 2010).

2 M. G. Shtein, *Ulianovy i Leniny: Tainy rodoslovnoi i psevdonima* (St Petersburg, 1997).

3 V. I. Lenin, *Polnoe sobranie sochinenii*, 5th edn (Moscow, 1958–65), vol. 47, p. 120; Lenin, *Collected Works* (Moscow, 1960–68), vol. 34, p. 372. Except where noted, I will use these two editions for Lenin quotations, so that the reader can consult either the Russian text or English translation. I will use the following style: Lenin, *pss* 47:120; *cw* 34:172. I take responsibility for all translations.

4 An example of this approach is Alfred G. Meyer, *Leninism* (New York, 1962).

5 The only reliable collection of new Lenin documents is *V. I Lenin, Neizvestnye dokumenty 1891–1922* (Moscow, 1999). Among the more important issues illuminated by new documents are Lenin's relations with Inessa Armand and with Roman Malinovsky, his attitude toward the Polish war as revealed in a speech of September 1920, and the events of his final months. Unfortunately, the English-language edition of the new documents is at a very low professional level; see my review of Richard Pipes, ed., *The Unknown Lenin: From the Secret Archive* (New Haven, CT, 1996) in *Canadian-American Slavic Studies*, XXXV/2–3 (Summer/Fall 2001), pp. 301–6 (one of the only reviews of the Pipes edition written after the Russian texts of the new documents had been

made available).

6 Michael Pearson, *Lenin's Mistress: The Life of Inessa Armand* (London, 2001). Helen Rappaport, author of the recent *Conspirator: Lenin in Exile* (London, 2009), has commented in an interview: 'There is, I am sure, a darker, sexual side to Lenin that has been totally suppressed in the Russian record. I do believe that whilst he was in Paris he went to prostitutes – there are clues in French sources about this, but it is very hard to prove.' See www.bookdepository.com/interview/with/author/helen-rappaport (accessed 5 May 2010).

7 Dmitri Volkogonov, *Lenin: A New Biography* (New York, 1994); Robert Service, *Lenin: A Biography* (Cambridge, MA, 2000). The only recent Lenin biography I can recommend with enthusiasm is Christopher Read, *Lenin* (London, 2005).

8 Lenin, *PSS* 49:378; *CW* 35:281.

9 *Vospominaniia o Vladimire Iliche Lenine* (Moscow, 1969), vol. 1, pp. 574–5.

10 Lenin *PSS* 6:107; Lars T. Lih, *Lenin Rediscovered: What Is to Be Done? in Context* (London, 2008), pp. 770–71 (in the case of *What Is to Be Done?* the references to an English-language source come from the translation of the entire book that is included in my study *Lenin Rediscovered*).

11 R. Tucker, *Political Culture and Leadership in Soviet Russia: From Lenin to Gorbachev* (New York, 1987), p. 39.

1 Another Way

1 Albert Rhys Williams, *Lenin: The Man and his Work* (New York, 1919), pp. 23–4.

2 M. G. Shtein, *Ulyanovy i Leniny: Tainy rodoslovnoi i psevdonima* (St Petersburg, 1997), pp. 43–7.

3 Katy Turton, *Forgotten Lives: The Role of Lenin's Sisters in the Russian Revolution, 1864–1937* (Basingstoke, 2007), p. 16.

4 Vladlen Loginov, *Vladimir Lenin: Vybor puti* (Moscow, 2005), p. 38.

5 My account of the 'second first of March' is based primarily on Norman Naimark, *Terrorists and Social Democrats: The Russian Revolutionary Movement under Alexander III* (Cambridge, MA, 1982). Phillip Pomper, *Lenin's Older Brother: The Origins of the October*

Revolution (New York, 2010) appeared too late for me to use.

6 *Narodnicheskaia ekonomicheskaia literatura*, ed. V. K. Karataev (Moscow, 1958), p. 634.

7 As cited in Paul Miliukov, *Russia and its Crisis* (London, 1962), p. 289 (originally published 1905).

8 The quoted words are from Marx's 1864 Inaugural Address for the International Working Men's Association.

9 John Rae, *Contemporary Socialism* (New York, 1884), pp. 127–9.

10 V. I. Lenin, *Polnoe sobranie sochinenii*, 5th edn (Moscow, 1958–65), vol. 41, p. 8; Lenin, *Collected Works* (Moscow, 1960–68), vol. 31, p. 25.

11 Loginov, *Vladimir Lenin*, p. 86.

12 Lenin, *PSS* 1:310, 330; *CW* 1:299, 318 (*Friends of the People*, 1894).

13 Lenin, *PSS* 1:333–4; *CW* 1:321 (*Friends of the People*, 1894).

14 Lenin, *PSS* 3:382; *CW* 3:382 (*Development of Capitalism in Russia*, 1899).

15 Cited by Lenin; see *PSS* 1:200; *CW* 1:197 (*Friends of the People*, 1894).

16 Cited by Lenin; see *PSS* 1:277–8, 282–3; *CW* 1:269, 273–4 (*Friends of the People*, 1894).

17 Boris Gorev, *Iz partiinogo proshlogo: Vospominaniia, 1895–1905* (Leningrad, 1924), pp. 7–9.

18 Vasily Vodovozov in *Na chuzhoi storone* (Prague, 1925), vol. 12, p. 177.

19 Lenin, *PSS* 1:200–202; *CW* 1:197–8 (*Friends of the People*, 1894).

20 Lenin, *PSS* 4:233; *CW* 4:248; Georgy Solomon, *Sredi krasnykh vozhdei* (Moscow, 1995), pp. 450–51. We should also note that the two major Russian Marxists of the time, Georgy Plekhanov and N. E. Fedoseev, both authority figures for the young Ulyanov, also reacted to the famine in complete contrast to the Mikhailovsky caricature.

21 Taken from Lenin's own summary in 1907 of the implications of his earlier book, *The Development of Capitalism* (published in 1899) (*PSS* 3:13; *CW* 3:31).

22 Lenin, *PSS* 55:1–2; *CW* 37:66 (letter of 5 October 1893).

23 Karl Kautsky, *Das Erfurter Programm* [1892] (Berlin, 1965), p. 250.

24 Ibid., p. 219.

25 Grigory Zinoviev, *Istoriia Rossisskoi Kommunisticheskoi Partii (bolshevikov)* (Leningrad, 1924), p. 116.

26 Lenin, *PSS* 1: 311–2; *CW* 1:300.

2 The Merger of Socialism and the Worker Movement

1   Boris Gorev, *Iz partiinogo proshlogo: Vospominaniia, 1895–1905* (Leningrad, 1924), p. 24.

2   V. I. Lenin, *Polnoe sobranie sochinenii*, 5th edn (Moscow, 1958–65), vol. 6, p. 152; Lars T. Lih, *Lenin Rediscovered: 'What Is to Be Done?' in Context* (Haymarket, 2008), p. 811.

3   Lenin, *PSS* 1:354–412; *CW* 1:340–95 (1894).

4   Lenin, *PSS* 46:12; *CW* 34:24 (letter of 16 August 1897).

5   Karl Kautsky, *Das Erfurter Programm* [1892] (Berlin, 1965).

6   Lenin, *PSS* 4:189; *CW* 4:217 (1899).

7   Lenin, *PSS* 2:101; *CW* 2:112 (1896).

8   Semën Kanatchikov, *A Radical Worker in Tsarist Russia: The Autobiography of Semën Ivanovich Kanatchikov*, ed. Reginald Zelnik (Stanford, CA, 1986), p. 70 (translation slightly modified). These memoirs were originally published in 1929. Kanatchikov puts the key phrases of his younger self and his comrades in quotes.

9   Ibid., p. 98.

10 From the so-called *Credo*, which evoked strong protests from Lenin and other Social Democrats; the full text can be found in Lenin *PSS* 4:165–9; *CW* 4:171–4 (1899).

11 Paul Miliukov, *Russia and its Crisis* [1905] (London, 1962), pp. 350–51.

12 Lenin, *PSS* 2:114; *CW* 2:125 (1896).

13 Lenin, *PSS* 2:300, 274; *CW* 2:302, 278 (1897).

14 Lenin, *PSS* 2:111–12; *CW* 2:123 (1896).

15 Lenin, *PSS* 2:460–61; *CW* 2:341–2 (1897).

16 Lenin's own words, from an unpublished biographical sketch written in 1917 (Lenin *PSS* 32:21).

17 Martov, *Zapiski Sotsial-demokrata* [1922] (Cambridge, MA, 1975).

18 Lenin, *PSS* 2:467; *CW* 2:348 (1897).

19 As cited in Miliukov, *Russia and its Crisis*, pp. 237–8.

20 Letter of 31 December 1928, written to the daughter of the deceased Inessa Armand, as published in *Izvestiia TSK KPSS*, 1989, no. 4, p. 184 (ellipsis in original).

21 Moissaye J. Olgin, *The Soul of the Russian Revolution* (New York, 1917), pp. 282–91.

22 M. Liadov, *Istoriia Rossiiskoi Sotsialdemokraticheskoi rabochei partii*

23 Lenin, *PSS* 2:458–65; *CW* 2:339–45.

24 Lenin, *PSS* 4:195–6; *CW* 4:223–4.

25 Martynov, 'Avtobiografiia', in *Deiateli SSSR i revoliutsionnogo dvizheniia Rossii: entsiklopedicheskii slovar' Granat* [1925–6] (Moscow, 1989), p. 525.

26 Lenin, *PSS* 2:268–9; *CW* 2:350 (1897).

27 K. N. Morozov, *Partiia sotsialistov-revoliutsionerov v 1907–1917 gg.* (Moscow, 1998), p. 40.

28 Lenin, *PSS* 6:132–3; Lih, *Lenin Rediscovered*, p. 794.

29 Pavel Axelrod, in a letter to Kautsky published in *Iskra*, 25 June 1904.

30 Aleksandr Nikolaevich Potresov, *Izbrannoe* (Moscow, 2002), pp. 67–120.

31 I. V. Stalin, *Sochineniia* (Moscow, 1946–52), vol. 4, pp. 308–9.

32 *Perepiska V. I. Lenina i redaktsii gazety 'Iskra' s sotsial-demokratich-eskimi organizatsiiami v Rossii, 1900–1903 gg.* (Moscow, 1969–70), vol. 2, pp. 28–9 (letter of 6 June 1902).

33 O. Piatnitsky, *Memoirs of a Bolshevik* [1925] (New York, n.d.), pp. 56–7.

34 Vladimir Ivanshin in *Rabochoe Delo*, No. 8 (November 1900), p. 11.

35 Lenin, *PSS* 6:107; Lih, *Lenin Rediscovered*, pp. 770–71.

36 Lenin, *PSS* 6:171; Lih, *Lenin Rediscovered*, p. 828.

3 A People's Revolution

1 This paraphrase of the meaning of *revoliutsiia do kontsa* comes from Bolshevik émigré Gregor Alexinsky in his still useful book *Modern Russia* (London, 1913), p. 254. In Lenin's *Collected Works*, the phrase *do kontsa* is translated in various ways, including 'through to victory' and 'to its [the revolution's] consummation'.

2 John W. Steinberg et al., eds, *The Russo-Japanese War in Global Perspective: World War Zero* (Leiden, 2005), 2 vols.

3 Zinoviev, *Sochineniia* (Moscow, 1923–4), vol. 15, p. 21 (from a 1918 biography of Lenin).

4 'Bolshevism as a tendency took definite shape in the spring and summer of 1905' (Lenin, *PSS* 19:364; *CW* 16:380) (1910). Axelrod's

letter to Kautsky was published in *Iskra* no. 68 (25 June 1904).

5 Lenin, *PSS* 9:126–36; *CW* 8:17–28.

6 M. Liadov, *Iz zhizni partii* (Moscow, 1956), p. 114 (originally published in 1926).

7 Lenin, *PSS* 12:336; *CW* 10:261 (1906).

8 Lenin, *PSS* 12:319; *CW* 10:245 (1906).

9 Lenin, *PSS* 17:49–50; *CW* 15:61 (1908).

10 Lenin, *PSS* 12:322; *CW* 10:248 (1906).

11 William English Walling, *Russia's Message: The True World Import of the Revolution* (New York, 1908); Walling, *Sovietism: The ABC of Russian Bolshevism – According to the Bolshevists* (New York, 1920).

12 Walling, *Russia's Message*, pp. 363–8.

13 Ibid., pp. 369–70.

14 L. Kamenev, 'The Literary Legacy and Collected Works of Ilyitch', from Marxists Internet Archive, www.marxists.org/archive/kamenev/19xx/x01/x01.htm (accessed 6 May 2010).

15 Lenin, *PSS* 49:413, *CW* 35:305 (letter of March 1917).

16 Lenin, *PSS* 16:329; *CW* 13:349. If pronouncements such as this were better known, the extreme democratism of *State and Revolution* (1917) would be less surprising.

17 Lenin, *PSS* 16:405, *CW* 13:423.

18 Lenin, *PSS* 16:325; *CW* 13:346.

19 Aleksandr Spiridovich, *Bol'shevizm: Ot zarozhdeniia do prikhoda k vlasti* (Moscow, 2005), p. 164 (originally published in 1922).

20 Ibid., pp. 164–7.

21 Ibid., p. 186.

22 Alexinsky, *Modern Russia*, p. 289.

23 Lev Kamenev, *Mezhdu dvumia revoliutsiiami* (Moscow, 2003), p. 560.

24 Lenin, *PSS* 17:31–2; *CW* 15:44 (1908).

25 Lenin, *PSS* 17:48–9; *CW* 15:60–61 (1908).

26 Lenin, *PSS* 12:339; *CW* 10:264 (1906).

27 Lenin, *PSS* 17:146; *CW* 15:156 (1908).

28 Leopold Haimson, 'Russian Workers' Political and Social Identities', in *Workers and Intelligentsia in Late Imperial Russia: Realities, Representations, Reflections*, ed. Reginald Zelnik (Berkeley, CA, 1999), p. 170. As Haimson points out, the Bolshevik devotion to the under-ground is not explainable by lack of success in legal, aboveground

institutions, since by the outbreak of war in 1914 the Bolsheviks were dominant in many of these legal organizations.

29 Lenin, *pss* 17:145; *cw* 15:154 (1908).

30 Lenin, *pss* 17:145 (1908); *cw* 15:20–21; see also *cw* 15:18, 290, 323 (1908).

31 Lenin *pss* 17:292; *cw* 15:288 (1908). Lenin refers specifically to the pamphlets issued during the revolution. 'According to the calculations of a competent bibliographist, between 1905 and 1907 no less than twenty-six million copies of books of pamphlets of Social Democratic tendencies were issued, and twenty-four millions of Revolutionary Socialist tendencies' (Gregor Alexinsky, *Modern Russia*, p. 262).

32 Georgy Solomon, *Sredi krasnykh vozhdei* (Moscow, 1995), p. 453.

33 Ibid., pp. 467–8. The fictional character Oblomov famously never managed to get out of bed for several hundred pages; Maria Tsebrikova (1835–1917) was a radical writer with a special interest in the woman question.

34 Substantial excerpts of this book can be found in Kamenev, *Mezhdu*, pp. 468–537.

35 Lenin, *pss* 48:308; *cw* 35:147 (letter of July 1914).

36 Lenin, *pss* 6:133; Lars T. Lih, *Lenin Rediscovered: 'What Is to Be Done?' in Context* (Haymarket, 2008), p. 794.

37 Lenin, *pss* 48:323; *cw* 43:423 (letter of July 1914).

38 Lenin, *pss* 20:387–8; *cw* 17:305 (December 1911).

39 Lenin, *pss* 23:296–305; *cw* 19:218–27.

40 *V. I. Lenin: Neizvestnye dokumenty, 1891–1922* (Moscow, 1999), p. 158 (letter of 12 July 1914).

4 Three Train Rides

1 V. I. Lenin, *Polnoe sobranie sochinenii*, 5th edn (Moscow, 1958–65), vol. 48, p. 330, *Collected Works* (Moscow, 1960–68), vol. 35, p. 154 (letter of 28 July 1914).

2 *Vladimir Ilich Lenin: Biograficheskaia Khronika* (Moscow, 1970–82), 12 vols, 3:267–8.

3 Lenin, *pss* 26:354; *cw* 21:342 (August 1915).

4 Lenin, *pss* 26:17–19; *cw* 21:29–30.

5 Lenin, *PSS* 27:76–81; *CW* 21:416–20.

6 For texts and background of the various anti-war resolutions of the Second International, see John Riddell, ed., *Lenin's Struggle for a Revolutionary International: Documents: 1907–1916, The Preparatory Years* (New York, 1984).

7 Lenin, *PSS* 27:102; *CW* 21:441 (January 1916).

8 Lenin, *PSS* 49:43–4; Olga Hess Gankin and H. H. Fisher, *The Bolsheviks and the World War: The Origin of the Third International* (Stanford, CA, 1940), p. 202 (letter to Kollontai, end of December 1914).

9 Gankin and Fisher, *Bolsheviks and the World War*, p. 460 (speech of 3 June 1916).

10 Lenin, *PSS* 49:20, 24; *CW* 35:167, 171 (letters to Alexander Shliapnikov from October 1914).

11 'Dead Chauvinism and Living Socialism' (December 1914), in Lenin, *PSS* 26:98–105; *CW* 21:94–101.

12 Karl Kautsky, *Road to Power*, trans. Raymond Meyer (Atlantic Highlands, NJ, 1996), pp. 88–91.

13 Lenin, *PSS* 49:82 (letter to Radek from June 1915); the pungent translation comes from R. Craig Nation, *War on War: Lenin, the Zimmerwald Left, and the Origins of Communist Internationalism* (Durham, NC, 1989), p. 78.

14 Lenin, *PSS* 49:82 (letter to Radek from June 1915).

15 Krupskaya, *Reminiscences of Lenin* (New York, 1960), p. 327.

16 Zinoviev, *Sochineniia* (Moscow, 1923–4), vol. 15, p. 39.

17 Lenin, *PSS* 27:48–51; *CW* 21:401–4.

18 In a lecture to Swiss workers given on 22 January 1917 Lenin insisted that 'we must not be deceived by the present grave-like stillness in Europe. Europe is pregnant with revolution'. He then went on to say 'We of the older generation may not live to see the decisive battles of this coming revolution.' This last statement is the basis for claims about Lenin's pessimism at this time. But Lenin is talking about socialist revolution in Europe as a whole, and his prediction is completely accurate: he did not live to see its decisive battles. Lenin, *PSS* 30:327–8, *CW* 23: 253.

19 Lenin, *PSS* 30:280; *CW* 23:211–2.

20 Lenin, *PSS* 49:390; *CW* 35:288.

21 N. Lénine and G. Zinoviev, *Contre le Courant*, vol. 2, trans. V. Serge

and Parijanine, n.d. (facsimile edition by Francis Maspero [Paris, 1970]), p. 112 (dated 31 January 1917).

22 For the theses of October 1915 see Lenin, *pss* 27:48–51; *cw* 21:401–4; for the theses of April 1917, see *pss* 31:113–18, *cw* 24:21–6.

23 Lenin, *pss* 49:421; *cw* 35:310 (letter to J. S. Hanecki, 30 March 1917).

24 Lenin, *pss* 31:55–7. Just before introducing the new goal of 'steps toward socialism', Lenin had read an article by Karl Kautsky on the prospects of the 1917 Russian revolution, and this article may have played the role of a catalyst in his thinking.

25 Lenin, *cw* 25:366; *pss* 34:200 (14 September 1917).

26 Lenin, *pss* 30:278–9; *cw* 23:210. The hope that wartime measures represented 'an instalment – a very large instalment – of Socialism' was a common one, as attested by these words of William Walling from 1915 in his *The Socialists and the War* (New York, 1972) (reprint of the 1915 edition), p. 500.

27 For *Threatening Catastrophe*, see Lenin, *pss* 34:151–99; *cw* 25:319–65. For *Can the Bolsheviks Retain State Power?* [*vlast*], see *pss* 34:287–339; *cw* 26:87–136.

28 Lenin, *pss* 34:159; *cw* 25:327.

29 Lenin, *pss* 34:315; *cw* 26:113.

30 Stalin, *Works* (Moscow, 1953), 3:275 (25 August 1917).

31 Lenin *pss* 35:2; *cw* 26:239. (Since the Russian Orthodox church did not accept the calendar reforms of Pope Gregory, the Russian Calendar was 13 days behind the European calendar by 1917. The new Bolshevik government switched to the European calendar in early 1918.)

32 For a detailed survey of the crises of 1918, see Alexander Rabinowitch, *The Bolsheviks in Power: The First Year of Soviet Rule in Petrograd* (Bloomington, IN, 2007).

33 *V. I. Lenin: Neizvestnye dokumenty, 1891–1922* (Moscow, 1999), pp. 246–7, 584–6 (details about the events in Penza are taken mainly from this source).

34 The texts of the relevant telegrams can be found in Lenin, *pss*, vol. 50; see particularly items 249, 254, 259, 261, 270. Despite the attention given to the telegram translated in the text, it adds very little to the picture provided by previously published material.

35 A. V. Peshekhonov, *Pochemu ia ne emigriroval* (Berlin, 1923), pp. 32–3

(the corpses were taken down for Christmas). For a synoptic view of non–Bolshevik terror, see G. A. Bordiugov, *Chrezvychainyi vek Rossiisskoi istorii: chetyre fragmenta* (St Petersburg, 2004), pp. 45–54. Terror of this sort was carried out not only by the White generals but party governments such as the SR-dominated Komuch in 1918.

36 Lenin, *PSS* 37:354; *CW* 28:340.
37 Lenin, *PSS* 37:305–31; *CW* 28:294–315.
38 Lenin, *PSS* 37:331; *CW* 28:318.
39 John Riddell, ed., *Founding the Communist International: Proceedings and Documents of the First Congress: March 1919* (New York, 1987), pp. 32, 302.
40 Arthur Ransome, *Russia in 1919* (New York, 1919), pp. 122–3; Krupskaya, *Reminiscences*, p. 488; *Vospominaniia o Vladimire Iliche Lenine* (Moscow, 1969), 1:533.
41 Lenin, *PSS* 38:215; *CW* 29:224–5 (March 1919).
42 Lenin, *PSS* 37:169–70; *CW* 28:165.

5 Beyond the 'Textbook à la Kautsky'

1 Lenin, 'Our Revolution', *Polnoe sobranie sochinenii*, 5th edn (Moscow, 1958–65), vol. 45, p. 382; Lenin, *Collected Works* (Moscow, 1960–68), vol. 33, p. 480. A 'textbook à la Kautsky' is something quite different from a 'Kautskyist textbook'. Since Lenin defined 'Kautskyism' as renegade behaviour, a 'Kautskyist textbook' could never be anything but harmful.
2 All of these phrases and more in the space of five pages (Lenin, *PSS* 45:378–82). Lenin's final writings have been conveniently published together with his major statements from 1922 by Pathfinder Press in *Lenin's Final Fight: Speeches and Writings, 1922–23* (New York, 1995). When appropriate, references to the English translation of Lenin's last writings will be made to this edition, cited as 'Pathfinder'; for 'Our Revolution', see Pathfinder, pp. 219–23.
3 Arthur Ransome, *Russia in 1919* (New York, 1919), p. 99 (in specific reference to trade unions).
4 Morris Hillquit, *From Marx to Lenin* (New York, 1921), pp. 113–14.
5 Leo Pasvolsky, *The Economics of Communism* (New York, 1921), p. 295.

6 William English Walling, *Sovietism* (New York, 1920), p. 52.

7 Muriel A. Payne, *Plague, Pestilence and Famine* (London, 1923), p. 48.

8 Ibid., pp. 75–6.

9 Ibid., pp. 36, 40.

10 Ibid., p. 138.

11 Ibid., pp. 142–3 (parenthetical comment inserted from earlier passage).

12 Ibid., p. xv; cf. p. 34. Payne's one mention of Lenin: 'The people absolutely worship Lenin – odd as this may seem in England. They don't seem to like Trotsky so much; but even the educated Russians never say a word against Lenin. There must be something in a man so much beloved' (p. 117).

13 My main source on the course of Lenin's health is the account of his sister Maria Ulyanova (published in *Izvestiia TSK KPSS*, 1991, nos 1–6).

14 Lenin, *PSS* 53:109 (letter of 9 August 1921).

15 Space does not permit a full analysis of a famous outburst in March 1922 in connection with a campaign to force the Orthodox Church to contribute some of its valuables to famine relief. Three summary points can be made: Lenin's outburst is not as bad as it is made to sound by the usual citations, often quoted without any context whatsoever; Lenin's more extreme rhetoric did *not* become as the basis of actual policy; the previous mitigating points still leave us with a repellent call for violence covered by a fig-leaf of legality. For the text of this memorandum, see *V. I. Lenin: Neizvestnye dokumenty, 1891–1922* (Moscow, 1999), pp. 516–19. For background on the expulsion of prominent intellectuals in 1922 see Stuart Finkel, *On the Ideological Front: The Russian Intelligentsia and the Making of the Soviet Public Sphere* (New Haven, CT, 2007).

16 Based on Maria Ulyanova's later account, as published in *Izvestiia TSK KPSS*, 1989, no. 12, p. 198; 1991, no. 3, p. 188. There is other documentary evidence that this conversation took place.

17 'Political Testament' was the title given to a recently published collection of letters by Engels (*Izvestiia TSK KPSS*, 1991, no. 6, p. 198).

18 *Izvestiia TSK KPSS*, 1991, no. 6, p. 197.

19 Ransome, *Russia in 1919*, pp. 118–19.

20 Ibid., p. 126. Ransome replied: yes, *abortive* typhoid.

21 Russell, *The Theory and Practice of Bolshevism*, 2nd edn (London, 1949) (first published 1920), p. 34. Lenin's scenario for England is set forth

in the pamphlet that he had just written for the Second Congress of the Third International, *Left-Wing Communism, A Sign of Growing Pains*.

22 For one example of such reassurances, see the speech of May 1919 (*Leninskii sbornik* [1970], 37:150).

23 Lenin, *PSS* 38:261–2; *CW* 29:271; see also *PSS* 38:316–19; *CW* 29:320–23.

24 Lenin, *PSS* 42:310–11; *CW* 32:113 (6 February 1921).

25 Lenin, *PSS* 44:293; *CW* 33:144–5 (23 December 1921).

26 Lenin, *PSS* 40:245; *CW* 30:450 (April 1920). Compare this claim to Lenin's bid for support from the middle peasant, as discussed later.

27 Lenin, *PSS* 45:401–6; Pathfinder, p. 251.

28 Lenin, *PSS* 44:79; *CW* 32:505 (letter to Ganka Miasnikov).

29 Lenin, *PSS* 38:256–8; *CW* 29:265–7.

30 Lenin, *PSS* 39:372–82; *CW* 30:193–204.

31 Lenin, *PSS* 42:180 (Eighth Congress of Soviets, December 1920).

32 Lenin, *PSS* 43:60–61; *CW* 32:216–17.

33 Lenin, *PSS* 38:194–5; *CW* 29:205 (speech at Eighth Party Congress, March 1919).

34 Lenin, *PSS* 42:195.

35 Pasvolsky, *Economics of Communism*, p. 265.

36 Lenin, *PSS* 38:200–201; *CW* 29:210–11 (Eighth Party Congress, March 1919) (Lenin's emphasis). See also *PSS* 38:29; *CW* 29:44–5 (March 1919).

37 Lenin, *PSS* 39:372–82; *CW* 30:193–204 (December 1919).

38 The metaphor of oases of collective production comes from N. Osinski in *Pravda*, 5 September 1920. For Lenin's electrification slogans see *PSS* 42:30; *CW* 31:419 (21 November 1920) and 42:157–9; *CW* 31:516 (22 December 1920).

39 Lenin, *PSS* 39:154; *CW* 29:555.

40 Lenin, *PSS* 40:230; *CW* 30:435 (from a short recorded speech). As Trotsky put it in February 1920, 'the grain will be returned to the village in several months, in a year or two, in the form of cloth, agricultural equipment, kerosene, and so on' (*Sochineniia* [Moscow, 1925–7], vol. 15, pp. 14–23).

41 Lenin, *PSS* 39:278; 30:113–14 (October 1919).

42 Lenin, *PSS* 43:29; *CW* 32:188–9 ('possibility of being his own boss' is a paraphrase of *svobodno khoziainichat*').

43 Lenin, 'On Cooperation', *PSS* 45: 369–77; Pathfinder, 209–18. During the Gorbachev era, this article was taken out of context and used to

advocate a move *away* from state control of distribution.

44 Instances of this phrase seem to be restricted to *PSS* 43:371 (notes for a speech to the Tenth Party Congress in 1921), *PSS* 44:160–1, *CW* 33: 65–6 (speech of October 1921); *PSS* 45:6, *CW* 33:216 (speech of 6 March 1922). Lenin also used similar expressions when discussing his fears that the party was being controlled by the bureaucracy (*PSS* 45:94–5; Pathfinder, pp. 50–51). Probably the hard-line connotations of the phrase arose when Stalin claimed that coercive collectivization had successfully solved the problem of *kto-kovo*.

45 Lenin *PSS* 45:383–88; Pathfinder, 233 ('How to Reorganize Rabkrin) (January 1923).

46 For example, *PSS* 38:62; *CW* 29:77 (March 1919).

47 Lenin *PSS* 41:27–8; *CW* 31:44–5 (summer 1920).

48 *Voprosy istorii KPSS*, 1990, no. 6, p. 33.

49 From Zinoviev's speech at the 8th Congress of Soviets, December 1920 (*Vosmoi vserossisskii s"ezd rabochikh, krestianskikh, krasnoarmeiskikh i kazachikh deputatov* (Moscow, 1921), pp. 207–12, 224.

50 Lenin, *PSS* 44:368–9.

51 Lenin, *PSS* 45:86; Pathfinder, p. 41 (speech in March 1922); cf. *PSS* 45:308, 390–91; Pathfinder, pp. 125, 238–9.

52 Lenin, *PSS* 45:95–100; Pathfinder, pp. 50–55. For capitalists worming their way into the bureaucracy and taking on the 'protective colouring' of Soviet employees, see *PSS* 39:155; *CW* 29:556 (August 1919).

53 Lenin's notes were published under the title 'Our Revolution' (*PSS* 45:378–82; Pathfinder, pp. 219–23).

54 Lenin, *PSS* 38:75; *CW* 29:95–6 (March 1919).

55 Lenin, 'How we should reorganize Rabkrin', *PSS* 45:383–8; Pathfinder, pp. 227–33.

56 Lenin, *PSS* 45:308; Pathfinder, pp. 124–5.

57 Lenin, *PSS* 45:406; Pathfinder, p. 252.

58 Lenin, *PSS* 45:363–8; Pathfinder, pp. 203–8 (published in *Pravda* on 4 January 1923).

59 Letter of 29 July 1923 (*Izvestiia TSK KPSS*, 1989, no. 4, pp. 186–7).

Epilogue

1 Grigory Zinoviev, *History of the Bolshevik Party* (London, 1973), p. 60.
2 Theodore Rothstein (a British socialist of Russian origin), originally in *The Social Democrat*, IX/2, February 1905, as reprinted in the Marxists Internet Archive, www.marxists.org/archive/rothstein/ 1905/02/russia.htm (accessed 7 May 2010).
3 V. I. Lenin, *Polnoe sobranie sochinenii*, 5th edn (Moscow, 1958–65), vol. 49, p. 340; Lenin, *Collected Works* (Moscow, 1960–68), vol. 35, p. 259 (letter of 18 December 1916).
4 Terry Pratchett, *Witches Abroad* (London, 1991). Katerina Clark's study of socialist realism reveals its close connection to Lenin's heroic scenario (*The Soviet Novel: History as Ritual*, Bloomington, IN, 2000); Ben Lewis's study asks some good questions about the Soviet *anekdot* (*Hammer and Tickle: The History of Communism Told Through Communist Jokes* [London, 2008]).
5 Robert C. Allen, *From Farm to Factory: A Reinterpretation of the Soviet Industrial Revolution* (Princeton, NJ, 2003), p. 131.
6 This observation comes from the so-called 'Riutin platform' (see *Reabilitatsiia* [Moscow, 1991], pp. 334–442).
7 Dmitri Pisarev, *Sochineniia* (Moscow, 1956), vol. 3, p. 148. For Lenin's citation of Pisarev, in *What Is to Be Done?*, see *PSS* 6:172; Lars T. Lih, *Lenin Rediscovered: 'What Is to Be Done?' in Context* (Haymarket, 2008), p. 829. Lenin's citation somewhat distorts Pisarev's actual argument.
8 Feodor Chaliapin, *Chaliapin, Man and Mask* (New York, 1932), p. 209.
9 Carter Elwood, 'What Lenin Ate', *Revolutionary Russia*, XX/2 (December 2007), pp. 137–49.
10 Leo Tolstoy, *Resurrection*, trans. Louise Maude (Oxford, 1994), pp. 435–7.
11 Georgy Solomon, S*redi krasnykh vozhdei* (Moscow, 1995), pp. 467–8.
12 *Istoricheskii arkhiv*, 1994, no. 4, pp. 11–18.
13 Nikolai Sukhanov, *The Russian Revolution of 1917* (Oxford, 1955), p. 290.
14 *1917: Chastnye svidetelstva o revoliutsii v pismakh Lunacharskogo i Martova* (Moscow, 2005), p. 126 (letter of January 1917).
15 Cited in Albert Rhys Williams, *Lenin: The Man and His Work* (New York, 1919), p. 67.

16 Cited by O. V. Shchelokov in *Mirovaia sotsial-demokratiia: teoriia, istoriia i sovremennost* (Moscow, 2006), p. 247 (Gorky's letter was first published in 1994). Lenin asked the party leadership to censure Gorky for his 1920 remark about Lenin's saintliness (Chris Read, *Lenin*, London, 2005, p. 260).

17 Unpublished jottings first published in *Izvestiia TSK KPSS*, 1989, No. 7, p. 171.

18 Nikolai Bukharin, *Ot krusheniia tsarizma do padeniia burzhuazii* [1917], (Kharkov, 1925), p. 60.

19 Arthur Ransome, *Russia in 1919* (New York, 1919), p. 122 (this interview took place during Lenin's 'anniversary' period from late 1918 to mid-1919).

20 Russell, *The Theory and Practice of Bolshevism* [1920], 2nd edn (London, 1949), p. 33.

Select Bibliography

Suggestions for Further Reading

Alexinsky, Gregor, *Modern Russia* (London, 1913)

Chamberlin, W. H., *The Russian Revolution, 1917–1921* [1935] (New York, 1965). 2 vols

Clark, Katerina, *The Soviet Novel: History as Ritual* (Bloomington, IN, 2000)

Donald, Moira, *Marxism and Revolution: Karl Kautsky and the Russian Marxists, 1900–1924* (New Haven, CT, 1993)

Elwood, Carter, *Inessa Armand: Revolutionary and Feminist* (Cambridge, 1992)

—, *Roman Malinovsky: A Life without a Cause* (Newtonville, MA, 1977)

—, 'What Lenin Ate', *Revolutionary Russia*, XX/2 (December 2007), pp. 137–49

Gankin, Olga Hess, and H. H. Fisher, *The Bolsheviks and the World War: The Origin of the Third International* (Stanford, CA, 1940)

Hillquit, Morris, *From Marx to Lenin* (New York, 1921)

Kamenev, Lev, 'The Literary Legacy and Collected Works of Ilyitch', from Marxists Internet Archive, www.marxists.org/archive/kamenev/19xx/x01/x01.htm (n.d.)

Kanatchikov, Semën, *A Radical Worker in Tsarist Russia: The Autobiography of Semën Ivanovich Kanatchikov*, ed. Reginald Zelnik (Stanford, CA, 1986)

Kautsky, Karl, *The Dictatorship of the Proletariat* [1918] (Ann Arbor, MI, 1964)

—, *Road to Power*, trans. Raymond Meyer (Atlantic Highlands, NJ, 1996)

Krupskaya, Nadezhda, *Reminiscences of Lenin* [1930] (New York, 1960)

Larsson, Reidar, *Theories of Revolution: From Marx to the First Russian Revolution* (Stockholm, 1970)

Lenin, V. I., *The Lenin Anthology*, ed. Robert Tucker (New York, 1974)

—, *Lenin's Final Fight: Speeches and Writings, 1922–23* (New York, 1995)

—, *Revolution at the Gates: A Selection of Writings from February to October 1917*, ed. Slavoj Zizek (London, 2002)

—, *Revolution, Democracy, Socialism*, ed. Paul Le Blanc (London, 2008)

Lih, Lars T., 'How a Founding Document was Found, or One Hundred Years of Lenin's What Is to be Done?', *Kritika* IV/1 (Winter 2003), pp. 1–45

—, 'Lenin and Kautsky, The Final Chapter', *International Socialist Review*, 59 (May–June 2008), available at www.isreview.org/issues/59/feat-lenin.shtml, accessed 10 May 2010

—, 'Lenin and the Great Awakening', in *Lenin Reloaded: Toward a Politics of Truth*, ed. Sebastian Budgen, Stathis Kouvelakis and Slavoj Zizek (Durham, NC, 2007)

—, *Lenin Rediscovered: 'What Is to Be Done?' in Context* (Haymarket, 2008)

—, 'Lenin's Aggressive Unoriginality, 1914–1916', *Socialist Studies: The Journal of the Society for Socialist Studies*, V/2 (Fall 2009), pp. 90–112

—, 'Political Testament of Lenin and Bukharin and the Meaning of NEP', *Slavic Review*, L/2 (Summer 1991), pp. 241–52

—, 'Zinoviev: Populist Leninist', *The NEP Era: Soviet Russia, 1921–1928*, II (2008), pp. 1–23

Lincoln, Bruce W., *Passage through Armageddon: The Russians in War and Revolution, 1914–1918* (New York, 1986)

—, *Red Victory: A History of the Russian Civil War* (New York, 1989)

Mandel, David, *The Petrograd Workers and the Fall of the Old Regime: From the February Revolution to the July Days, 1917* (London, 1983)

—, *The Petrograd Workers and the Soviet Seizure of Power: From the July Days, 1917 to July 1918* (London, 1984)

Miliukov, Paul, *Russia and its Crisis* [1905] (London, 1962)

Naimark, Norman, *Terrorists and Social Democrats: The Russian Revolutionary Movement under Alexander III* (Cambridge, MA, 1982)

Nation, R. Craig, *War on War: Lenin, the Zimmerwald Left, and the Origins of Communist Internationalism* (Durham, NC, 1989)

Olgin, Moissaye J., *The Soul of the Russian Revolution* (New York, 1917)

Pasternak, Boris, *Dr Zhivago* (London, 1958)

Pasvolsky, Leo, *The Economics of Communism* (New York, 1921)

Pearson, Michael, *The Sealed Train* (New York, 1975)

Piatnitsky, O., *Memoirs of a Bolshevik* (New York, n.d.)

Pomper, Phillip, *Lenin's Older Brother: The Origins of the October Revolution* (New York, 2010)

Rabinowitch, Alexander, *The Bolsheviks Come to Power: The Revolution of 1917 in Petrograd* (Chicago, 2004)

—, *The Bolsheviks in Power: The First Year of Soviet Rule in Petrograd* (Bloomington, IN, 2007)

Ransome, Arthur, *The Crisis in Russia* (New York, 1921)

—, *Russia in 1919* (New York, 1919)

Read, Chris, *Lenin* (London, 2005)

Riddell, John, ed., *Founding the Communist International: Proceedings and Documents of the First Congress: March 1919* (New York, 1987)

—, ed., *Lenin's Struggle for a Revolutionary International: Documents: 1907–1916, The Preparatory Years* (New York, 1984).

—, ed., *Workers of the World and Oppressed Peoples, Unite!: Proceedings and Documents of the Second Congress, 1920* (New York, 1991)

Russell, Bertrand, *The Theory and Practice of Bolshevism* [1920] (2nd edn, London, 1949)

Sholokhov, Mikhail, *Quiet Flows the Don*, translated by Robert Daglish, revd and ed. Brian Murphy (London, 1996)

Steinberg, John W. et al., eds, *The Russo–Japanese War in Global Perspective: World War Zero* (Leiden, 2005), 2 vols

Sukhanov, Nikolai, *The Russian Revolution of 1917* [1922–3] (Oxford, 1955)

Tucker, Robert, *Political Culture and Leadership in Soviet Russia: From Lenin to Gorbachev* (New York: 1987)

Turton, Katy, *Forgotten Lives: The Role of Lenin's Sisters in the Russian Revolution, 1864–1937* (Basingstoke, 2007)

Vihavainen, Timo, *The Inner Adversary: The Struggle against Philistinism as the Moral Mission of the Russian Intelligentsia* (Washington, DC, 2006)

von Laue, Theodore, *Why Lenin? Why Stalin? A Reappraisal of the Russian Revolution, 1900–1930* (Philadelphia, PA, 1964)

Wade, Rex, *The Russian Revolution 1917* (Cambridge, 2000)

Walling, William English, *Russia's Message: The True World Import of the Revolution* (New York, 1908)

—, *Sovietism: The ABC of Russian Bolshevism – According to the Bolshevists* (New York, 1920)

Weber, Hermann, and Gerda Weber, *Lenin: Life and Works* (London, 1980)

Zinoviev, Grigory, *History of the Bolshevik Party* [1923] (London, 1973)

Filmography (all available on DVD)

Doktor Zhivago, dir. Alexander Piroshkin (2005) (Russian TV series)

The End of St Petersburg, dir. Vsevolod Pudovkin (1927)

Mother, dir. Vsevolod Pudovkin (1926)

October (Ten Days that Shook the World), dir. Sergei Eisenstein (1927)

Quiet Flows the Don, dir. Sergei Gerasimov (1957)

Storm Over Asia, dir. Vsevolod Pudovkin (1928)

Strike, dir. Sergei Eisenstein (1924)

Three Songs about Lenin, dir. Dziga Vertov (1934)

Acknowledgements

My thanks to Esther Leslie for suggesting my name as a contributor to the excellent Critical Lives series; thanks also to Michael Leaman and Reaktion Books for patient and (when needed) not-so-patient encouragement. My thinking about Lenin has been greatly influenced by discussions over the past few years with many colleagues, too numerous to mention, but all equally committed to 'the search for the historical Lenin'. The first draft of the present book underwent a close and critical reading by Julie Cumming; later drafts benefited from the comments of Barbara Allen, Paul Le Blanc, Manny Ness, Erik van Ree, and Ron Suny. The final draft received a much-needed once-over from Ariadne Lih.

This book is dedicated to Julie Cumming, Emelyn Lih, Ariadne Lih, and to the memory of Morgana.